the **NO-NONSENSE** guide to

THE A...E

VS

'Publishers have created lists of short books that discuss the questions that your average [electoral] candidate will only ever touch if armed with a slogan and a soundbite. Together [such books] hint at a resurgence of the grand educational tradition... Closest to the hot headline issues are *The No-Nonsense Guides*. These target those topics that a large army of voters care about, but that politicos evade. Arguments, figures and documents combine to prove that good journalism is far too important to be left to (most) journalists.'

Boyd Tonkin,
The Independent,
London

The No-Nonsense Guide to The Arms Trade
First published in the UK by
New Internationalist™ Publications Ltd
Oxford OX4 1BW, UK
www.newint.org
New Internationalist is a registered trade mark.

in association with
Verso
6 Meard Street
London
W1F 0EG
www.versobooks.com

Cover image: Italian Aermacchi S-211 fighter jet, at the Paris Air Show
1992, with unguided rockets (center) and 500-lb bombs. The jets have
been sold to Singapore, the Philippines and other air forces.
George Hall / Corbis

Design by New Internationalist Publications Ltd.
Series editor: Troth Wells

Printed by TJ International Ltd, Padstow, Cornwall, UK.

British Library Cataloguing-in-Publication Data.
A catalogue record for this book is available from the British Library.

Library of Congress Cataloguing-in-Publication Data.
A catalogue for this book is available from the Library of Congress.

ISBN 1-85984-426-X

the **NO-NONSENSE** guide to
THE ARMS TRADE

Gideon Burrows

About the author
Gideon Burrows is a London-based journalist and campaigner. He has been campaigns co-ordinator of the UK's Campaign Against Arms Trade (CAAT), is actively involved in the peace and anti-arms trade movement and is a conscientious objector to paying taxes for military purposes. He writes on human rights, development, the environment, peace, civil liberties, trade unionism and the global justice movement. His website address is at www.foundationspa.co.uk.

Acknowledgements
Special thanks to all at CAAT for help and support, especially to Martin, Emily and the Mole for always impressing and inspiring me. Thanks to Troth Wells for ideas and encouragement, and Yvonne Ridley for being so keen on the project.

Foreword

I HAVE DEVOTED my energy since September 11 2001 working for peace and justice at a time when many countries, including America and Britain, are dropping bombs and preparing for more wars. In that time I have spoken to scores of Afghan landmine victims who've lost limbs – innocent men, women and children who happened to be in the wrong place at the wrong time.

I have spoken to frustrated Afghan farmers who want to plough their fields and produce food to feed their families but are unable to because the soil is littered with deadly cluster bombs... the yellow, box-shaped bombs which were dropped in the same area the US dropped yellow boxes containing peanut jelly and other non-*halal* food for the Islamic country's starving people.

My work has also taken me to Palestine, through the rubble of Ramallah and Nablus. I have witnessed the devastation caused by military might against the unarmed people of the Jenin refugee camp in May 2002. When the Israelis attacked Jenin, home to 13,000 defenseless Palestinians, they used F-16 fighter jets to drop bombs, fired missiles from Apache attack helicopters and used tanks to shell and demolish homes. As I left the chaos and carnage in Jenin the people were still digging through the wreckage to find their loved ones.

The whole world watches nervously as tensions increase between Pakistan and India, both nuclear powers, as they squabble over Kashmir. But perhaps the most shocking sight was the inside of the Al-Amirayeh bomb shelter where 408 Iraqi women and children perished in 1991 during the Gulf War. The sight of tiny fingers and toes, petrified to the metal ceiling, will haunt me forever.

George W Bush, a man sitting in the White House who many say was not democratically elected, says he will attack Iraq because he wants to depose Saddam Hussein, a man that no-one elected. Such a war will mean more bombs, more weapons, and more needless deaths.

All these atrocities have a common thread. They were caused by deadly weapons produced around the world. When weapons are fired in anger it is a terrible fact that they often target innocent civilians. Politicians and the military brush these sad statistics aside using gross euphemisms like 'collateral damage'. Yet as they shed their crocodile tears they continue to sell or to buy more weapons to feed the never-ending war machine. Most of the arms deals are said to be perfectly legal and acceptable, yet in this book Gideon Burrows has also unearthed the shenanigans that come from the illicit arms market which co-exists in a parallel universe.

This book highlights some striking ironies including, for instance, the case of Afghanistan where the arms have outlasted the political relationships that exist between the supplier and the recipient. (For supplier include the CIA and for recipient add Osama bin Laden).

This *No-Nonsense Guide to The Arms Trade* gives a chilling insight in to how the arms trade works and how the deals are cut long before the weapons are deployed.

Yvonne Ridley
Journalist and writer,
London

Yvonne Ridley was seized by the Taliban in Afghanistan, after the attacks of 11 September 2001 in the US, while reporting for the UK's *Sunday Express* and *Daily Express* newspapers from Pakistan.

the **NO-NONSENSE** guide to
THE ARMS TRADE

CONTENTS

the **NO-NONSENSE** guide to

THE ARMS TRADE

MOST PEOPLE REMEMBER where they were on 11 September 2001, when they first heard that terrorists had flown planes into the World Trade Center and the Pentagon in the United States. I was with more than a thousand other people in south London, protesting outside the biggest ever arms exhibition to take place on British soil, Defence Systems Equipment International (DSEi).

In the late afternoon, police asked us if we were going to cancel protests for the rest of the week as a mark of respect. One officer told me we were 'sick for continuing to be here after what happened'. We inquired whether the arms fair would also cease its business, just as many other events across the world had been cancelled, in reaction to the attacks.

DSEi 2001 was not cancelled. For four more days, arms buyers from the US, Israel and 14 different Arab nations rubbed shoulders inside the heavily protected exhibition center, shopping for guns, bombs, weapons electronics, anti-tank mines, cluster munitions, fighter jets, tanks and untold other armaments. Sworn enemies shopped side by side for weapons to use against one another.

On the morning of writing, I attended the Annual General Meeting of one of the world's biggest arms companies, BAE Systems – my single 'token' share granting me access. After being filled with coffee and biscuits, we were ushered into a plush conference suite and spun seemingly endless speeches about how well the company was doing, and what a socially responsible firm it was.

We put our questions to the board: about human rights, conflict, third world debt and development; about bribery and corruption, political influence and disproportionate government subsidies; and we asked about the arms trade's possible role in creating the circumstances which led to the September 11 attacks. Every question – most matters of life and death – were shrugged off, ignored, or answered in a misleading and obtuse way. The arms business in today's world has a friendly, respectable face, but it is as murky, secretive and amoral as it has always been.

This *No-Nonsense Guide to The Arms Trade* attempts to give some background to those questions, answer a few, and provide campaigners and others with material for more questions to arms companies, governments and the military complex the world over. It is a work of passion, rather than a textbook. Its value is as a tool for spreading information and for future campaigning.

The world is much smaller today, thanks to globalization, with arms companies becoming bigger even than countries. The response of activists has to be similar, if we are to keep up the pressure, linking up with other movements, campaigners and individuals pressing non-violently for peace, justice and a fairer world.

To anyone who asks, 'what is the point?', I have only one reply. We must keep pushing the issues because if we do not, who knows what could happen next. Who knows how many more Tiananmen Squares, East Timors, or Congos would have taken place had not campaigners agitated for arms sales to be restricted, and for action to bring a more just and stable world.

To borrow, but turn around, the weak old challenge of the arms business, 'if we don't sell arms, someone else will': if we do not keep up the questioning, challenging, direct action, protesting and political lobbying, are we sure someone else would?

Gideon Burrows
London

1 Overview of the global arms trade

A picture of the trade, and the countries and companies that are the main players... Who buys and who sells?... The problems of licensed production and small arms.

I HAD JUST gone through security at the Eurosatory 2000 arms fair in Paris, my heart was pounding but I was relieved. I waited, on the other side of the security area, for my colleague, another anti-arms trade campaigner. After 10 minutes he hadn't arrived. I ventured gingerly back into the security area to see where he had got to, only to see him being led away by security.

My colleague had been picked up by the arms fair's banned list – his name had flashed up on the screen as someone not to be allowed into the fair. More surprising, though, was that I had got through and he hadn't.

Then it came to me – not being a French speaker, I had written my last name in the wrong place on the security form. My name was Burrows Gideon, according to my pass, and the computer hadn't picked me up.

They say ignorance is bliss. As I ventured into that Paris arms fair to view the guns, planes, bombs and tanks, I wished it was... at least sometimes.

The business of buying and selling arms has changed hugely over the last 25 years. For the majority of the 20th century, right up until the final years of the Cold War, arms companies were essentially national assets manufacturing weapons systems, arms and other equipment to meet domestic need.

The companies were intimately involved in the defense ambitions of their host country. They were often state-owned, usually inseparable from the country's own armed forces, and strategically connected to their host country's international, national and military enterprises. From the end of the 1950s, the majority of overseas arms transfers were either sold or donated to strategic partners drawn along Cold War lines. Some other overseas arms sales did take place, chiefly to countries with some military need but no established arms industry, but only to lengthen local production lines and so reduce the unit cost of the weapons for the host government.

For the most part, states paid for and carried out military research themselves and awarded contracts to domestic arms companies to meet mainly their own, and their allies, defense needs.

With the development of international relations following the Second World War and the strengthening of alliances in the Cold War environment, a few cross-border weapons manufacturing projects were undertaken. Britain and France built the Jaguar strike plane in the 1970s, and Britain, Germany and Italy linked up to build the Tornado jet fighter in the 1980s.

But political implications, worries over national security and secrecy, and the practical problems of getting everything to fit together stalled many projects for decades and stopped others in their early stages.

The end of Cold War tensions in the late 1980s, and the collapse of the USSR, soon changed the world arms market beyond recognition. The main result was a great reduction in the global demand for military equipment. Worldwide military expenditure has fallen steadily since 1987, with only a minor increase when Western nations rearmed following the Gulf tensions in the 1990s. Between 1987 and 1997, global military expenditure fell by one-third, with the steepest reduction in the former Soviet Union. Military spending among NATO member states declined by just under a quarter in the same period, and is only very recently beginning to climb again.[1]

The Stockholm International Peace Research Institute (SIPRI) records that the volume of military imports of major conventional weapons, such as planes, tanks and explosive systems was, at constant 1990 prices, \$15,333 million in 2000, compared with \$19,213 million in 1995, and \$23,582 million in 1991.[2]

An international business

Coupled with progress in technology and better international communications, the reduction in the global demand for arms has resulted in an industry forced to consolidate across international boundaries. The consolidating countries sought to develop their market by 'scenario setting' to identify potential enemies and allies, from which emerged the concept of 'rogue states' against whom Western countries and their allies had to arm.

As governments detached themselves from state arms companies, and reduced spending on military research, weapons producers became relatively independent commercial concerns, though still receiving hefty subsidies from their host countries. In the search for a slice of a shrinking cake, they sought out economically strategic partnerships and pursued new markets including the oil-rich Middle East, Asia and Southeast Asia.

No longer intimately linked to national security, a

Whose figures for military expenditure?

The arms trade is a notoriously secretive business: no surprise when countries want to protect their national security by keeping hidden the details of what they buy from potential future enemies.

In addition, the pricing of weapons and weapons systems varies according to currency fluctuations, commissions, off-set arrangements and profit margins. Of course, it also depends on who is giving you the figures.

As a result, it is virtually impossible to achieve accurate statistics for the military expenditure for one country, let alone worldwide. For the purposes of continuity, figures for military expenditure for countries and worldwide in this chapter are taken as recorded by the Stockholm International Peace Research Institute (SIPRI), which has an excellent reputation and consistent research methods. ■

country's arms companies were able to bid in open competition for contracts with nations that had developed armaments industries of their own. The process forced down profit margins and further increased the need for arms companies to merge to create international integrated business, or go into sourcing relationships with smaller second-tier suppliers, in order to survive.

The huge costs of modern military equipment and declining demand meant that a small number of Western companies became premier league transnationals in the business, accelerating their expansion by gobbling up smaller companies in secondary countries. So, for example, Thales (the renamed French Thomson-CSF) has bought companies in Australia, South Africa, and Korea, opening up access to those markets for its products.

As Stephen Staples, a founder member of the International Network on Disarmament and Globalization (INDG), writes: 'Former nationally orientated defense companies such as Boeing, GM and BAE Systems (formerly British Aerospace – BAe) are now transnational corporations that roam the world in search of higher government subsidies and tax incentives, lower wages and weaker labor standards.'[3]

Yet arms manufacturers necessarily remain in close collusion with states. Their products are still national assets, and their only customers are governments. States still use their arms industries as a diplomatic tool in international relations, granting arms deals with other nations as part of wider agreements.

Thus the arms trade, as it appears today, is unique in terms of international business – it consists of transnational companies that are still jealously treasured as national assets by the countries from which they sprang, receiving special treatment, political and financial support. Yet they are only nominally subject to the legal, tax and moral obligations of their host countries.

Big hitters

The top 20 suppliers of major conventional weapons from 1996 to 2000. Figures are trend-indicator* values, expressed in US $m at constant (1990) prices.

1996-2000	Supplier	1996	1998	2000	1996-2000
1	US	9,160	12,970	5,489	**49,271**
2	Russia	3,309	1,595	4,443	**15,690**
3	France	1,833	3,370	1,040	**10,792**
4	UK	1,477	1,037	1,035	**7,026**
5	Germany	1,418	1,201	1,235	**5,647**
6	Netherlands	397	579	183	**2,014**
7	Ukraine	202	615	67	**1,956**
8	Italy	389	347	177	**1,720**
9	China	652	285	54	**1,506**
10	Belarus	113	58	498	**1,246**
11	Spain	79	167	51	**945**
12	Israel	200	136	212	**864**
13	Canada	189	140	85	**716**
14	Australia	14	3	5	**646**
15	Sweden	150	116	137	**585**
16	Switzerland	125	31	60	**340**
17	Czech Republic	140	20	87	**340**
18	Moldova	–	–	–	**316**
19	Belgium	145	23	–	**285**
20	Slovakia	48	8	91	**196**

*The SIPRI data on arms transfers refer to actual deliveries of major conventional weapons. To permit comparison between the data on such deliveries of different weapons and identification of general trends, SIPRI uses a 'trend indicator value'. The SIPRI values are only an indicator of the volume of international arms transfers and not of the actual financial values of such transfers.

SIPRI Yearbook 2001, Stockholm International Peace Research Institute, June 2001.

Who sells the weaponry?

Unsurprisingly, the West dominates the world arms market in terms of sales. Over the last six or so years, the US has towered over the other countries in weapons sales, clocking up $49,271 million worth of sales (at 1990 prices) between 1996 and 2000.[4] Its nearest competitor, Russia, made $15,690 million worth in the same period, but a large majority of these were of second hand weapons.

According to SIPRI, just under half of all transfers

(movements) of major conventional weapons between 1996 and 2000 came from the US. Russia and France each accounted for 10 per cent, and Britain and Germany each accounted for between five and 10 per cent. The seven following biggest sellers – the Netherlands, Ukraine, Italy, China, Belarus, Spain and Israel – accounted for around 15 per cent of the world total transfers between them.

So it is clear that the global arms market is controlled by just a few players. The six biggest arms selling countries – four of whom, ironically, are permanent members of the UN Security Council – accounted for almost 85 per cent of all arms transfers over the last six years.

Within those countries, and across their borders, stretch a handful of huge armaments companies and hundreds of very small components and specialist manufacturers.

The biggest arms corporations originated in the US, and still call North America home. Those that started operations in Europe are less tied to their country of birth – but remain distinctly European. As yet there are only a few Euro-American weapons conglomerates like Tracor and BAE Systems North America (the US Department of Defense treats them as US companies), and there are numerous strategic partnerships; the British BAE Systems is strongly US-focused.

The big hitters' world ranking fluctuates from year to year, and accurate statistics are difficult to obtain and compare. SIPRI paints a picture in 1999 which shows that the US Lockheed Martin company – a specialist in war planes as well as civil airliners – leading the field in terms of sales, with $17.6 billion of sales during 1999. Military equipment made up around 70 per cent of the company's sales in that year.

Boeing is its closest local military equipment manufacturing competitor, but the company itself is much larger – weapons sales made up only 27 per cent of total sales that year. According to SIPRI, BAE Systems

Military might

The top 7 largest arms companies, in terms of military sales. The figures in *italics* represent the percentage of arms in total sales for each company. Figures for arms sales are in US $ billions at constant (1998) prices and exchange rates.

Company, country	1994	1995	1996	1997	1998	1999
Lockheed Martin (US)	15.9 *63*	14.8 *60*	18.7 *67*	18.8 *66*	17.9 *68*	17.6 *70*
BAE Systems (UK)	9.1 *62*	8.2 *68*	9.4 *72*	10.9 *74*	10.5 *74*	15.7 *77*
Boeing (US)	4.5 *18*	4.5 *22*	4.2 *18*	14.7 *32*	15.9 *28*	15.3 *27*
Raytheon (US)	3.9 *35*	4.2 *34*	4.7 *37*	5.2 *37*	12.5 *64*	11.3 *58*
Northrop Grumman (US)	6.2 *85*	6.1 *84*	7.0 *83*	7.3 *79*	6.7 *75*	7.0 *79*
General Dynamics (US)	3.2 *94*	3.2 *96*	3.4 *92*	3.7 *90*	4.2 *84*	5.5 *62*
Thomson-CSF (France)	4.2 *65*	4.1 *65*	4.0 *64*	4.2 *64*	4.6 *63*	4.1 *56*

SIPRI Yearbook 2001, Stockholm International Peace Research Institute, June 2001.

(having acquired its main UK rival GEC) was the second largest arms seller in 1999, with $15.7 billion sales – 77 per cent of its business.

The other major-league weapons producers are Raytheon (US), General Dynamics (US), EADS (France/Germany/Spain), Northrop Grumman (US) and Thales, formerly Thomson-CSF (France).

Who buys the weapons?

It is when one glances at the list of the main purchasers of weapons that the problem of the arms trade really begins to emerge. The top 20 arms buyers, over the last five years, according to SIPRI, include human rights-abusing states like Saudi Arabia, Turkey and China; and countries in military tension with another such as South Korea, India, Greece, Israel and Pakistan. Different countries do, of course, have traditional suppliers, mainly as a hangover from Cold War alliances.

Taiwan, Saudi Arabia, Turkey, United Arab Emirates and South Korea were the biggest buyers of arms over the last 10 years. But recent studies by the Congressional Research Service on behalf of the US Congress reveal that arms sales to Third World nations are steadily increasing and together far outweigh arms sales to developed countries. According to their figures, developing or majority world countries accounted for 66 per cent of the value of all international arms deliveries in 2000. Between 1997 and 2000,

Buying fire-power

The top 20 arms-purchasing countries between 1996 and 2000. Figures are trend-indicator* values expressed in US $ millions, at constant (1990) prices.

1996-2000	Recipient	1996	1998	2000	1996-2000
1	Taiwan	1,313	4,022	445	**12,281**
2	Saudi Arabia	1,728	2,529	92	**8,362**
3	Turkey	1,143	1,766	704	**5,664**
4	South Korea	1,566	870	708	**5,334**
5	China	1,047	88	2,085	**5,231**
6	India	804	547	429	**4,228**
7	Greece	262	1,467	462	**3,665**
8	Egypt	918	515	580	**3,619**
9	Japan	501	1,236	190	**3,558**
10	UAE	549	843	280	**2,983**
11	Israel	75	1,300	270	**2,890**
12	Finland	564	565	443	**2,787**
13	Pakistan	476	579	206	**2,626**
14	Kuwait	1,240	191	104	**2,063**
15	Singapore	512	654	412	**1,874**
16	Thailand	604	59	84	**1,771**
17	UK	235	379	866	**1,694**
18	Switzerland	199	459	46	**1,612**
19	Malaysia	49	37	52	**1,445**
20	Brazil	453	145	244	**1,346**

*The SIPRI data on arms transfers refer to actual deliveries of major conventional weapons. To permit comparison between the data on such deliveries of different weapons and identification of general trends, SIPRI uses a 'trend indicator value'. The SIPRI values are only an indicator of the volume of international arms transfers and not of the actual financial values of such transfers.

SIPRI Yearbook 2001, Stockholm International Peace Research Institute, June 2001.

the figure was 70.2 per cent, and in the four years prior to that, it was 65.9 per cent.[5]

The arms trade in international relations

Despite the growth of private arms companies from former state-owned firms, the arms business remains inseparable from the political movements of today's world. As alliances are struck between nations and across continents, as agreements are signed and incorporated into domestic legislation, the arms industry plays an important and strategic part. World politics can be compared to a board game, with world leaders as the players and arms companies as their willing pawns. Some argue it is the other way around. Companies are instrumental in 'scenario setting' to identify potential enemies, and there is a blurred boundary between government and corporations (see chapter 7).

Are women pawns or players in the war game?

Women are the majority of the world's refugees fleeing the violence of interstate wars with their dependent children.

Think about the words 'women' and 'war'. Chances are another word will soon flash across your mind: victim. This is to be expected. Four out of five victims of war today are civilians – and most of them are female.

During the Gulf War in 1992-2 women in their camouflage fatigues kept appearing in our magazines and on our TV screens. Although women have supported regular armies of warring states for the past 80 years, this war was the first in which they played such a central role in soldiering. Thousands served as troop deployment planners. They attracted a lot of media attention precisely because they overturned the stereotype of the female victim of war.

Interviewers wanted to know how they were handling chauvinism in their mostly male crews? Did they expect to be in a combat zone? Did they worry about being good wives and mothers to the families they had left back home? In their quest for equality, women were becoming more receptive to militaristic ideas. Many believed they could win first-class citizenship the way men can by serving in the uniformed military – in spite of all the contrary evidence of sexual harassment and discrimination.

The fact is women are very vulnerable to military values and beliefs even though these rarely, if ever, serve their long-term interests. This vulnerability is crucial – for if women stopped giving support the system

Joint weapons programs have solidified European alliances. Britain, Germany, Italy and Spain have collaborated to produce a common fighter aircraft – the Eurofighter (export name, Typhoon). France and Germany collaborated to create the Eurocopter company, which has also co-opted Agusta of Italy and Fokker of the Netherlands to make a new series of naval helicopters.

The so-called 'special relationship' between the US and Britain has also been punctuated by collaborative arms projects, most starkly the Joint Strike Fighter (JSF), which will produce up to 3,000 fighter planes for the United Sates and up to 150 for Britain. Exports of 3,000 more are hoped for.

British giant BAE Systems (which has special access, usually only granted to US companies, to the Pentagon) has a large stake in manufacture of JSF, led

would collapse.

In a mere five days after America's launch of the air war against Baghdad, US women's opposition to their government's resort to force went down from over 40 per cent to a little over 20 per cent. Why and how did so many women start supporting military policy-makers, despite the fact that militarization robs women not only of physical security but of political influence too?

Ironically, it Is because women are oppressed that they end up internalizing and supporting military values and beliefs. They do not espouse these in a vacuum but in the process of trying to live up to their society's standards of femininity.

If women cannot be the fighters themselves they can at least prove their patriotism by urging their sons to enlist, or by coping proudly with war-caused food shortages.

In their everyday lives women all over the world are both victims and participants in the militarization game. It presents us with many dilemmas. For example, how does someone aspiring to be a good mother show support for her soldier son or daughter without voicing support for her government's use of armed force?

Recognizing women as both victims and participants may cause unease. But focussing on everyday examples helps us realize what a contradictory thing militarism is – and how much it relies upon women to maintain it. This could lead us on to developing ways of opposing it. ∎

Cynthia Enloe, *New Internationalist*, Issue 221 July 1991.

by Lockheed Martin. The British are the only full col-
laborators in the project, though the Netherlands,
Belgium, Denmark, Norway, Canada, Italy, Israel,
Turkey and Singapore all have lesser stakes in it.

As Chris Wrigley, a researcher for the UK organization Campaign Against Arms Trade (CAAT), writes in
his pamphlet *The Arms Industry*: 'The real point is that
the Joint Strike Fighter is essentially a US plane,
designed to be the main instrument of US global hegemony in the next generation. The [British] Royal Navy
will have a small share of the output, and so of the
hegemony.'[6]

The European Framework Agreement
and the EU Code of Conduct

CAAT has argued that the continued existence of the
North Atlantic Treaty Organization (NATO) is influenced by the wish to facilitate arms sales to existing
and new members.

'The prospect of NATO membership gives a power-
ful boost to local militarists. Collusion between
Western arms companies, the armed forces and the
depressed local arms industries is likely to lead to eastern Europe being filled with expensive fleets of
state-of-the-art warplanes and much other pointless
military hardware,' says one CAAT report.[7]

It is certainly within the intentions of the main
European nations to smooth arms purchasing
between themselves and to improve joint working,
thereby strengthening Europe as a region in terms of
military might, economic independence and political
significance. The arms companies have their own
interests in growth, allegiances and market share.

In 2000, six European nations finalized details of an
agreement to smooth arms purchasing and weapons
manufacturing collaboration between them. The
*Framework Agreement Concerning Measures to Facilitate the
Restructuring and Operation of the European Defense
Industry*, signed on 27 July 2000 by Britain, Germany,

France, Sweden, Italy and the Netherlands, is as complicated as it sounds.

The Agreement outlined common research, development and supply of joint weapons projects between the signatory countries. But it also established protocols for exporting those weapons outside the group of six. Campaigners lobbied against the Agreement, arguing that it would reduce transparency and accountability of arms exports from member countries.

Under the Framework Agreement, signatories collaborating on an arms project would draw up a list of countries to which they wished to export the system. The list would not be open to scrutiny by elected parliamentarians in the member states, let alone the general public. Also, arms export licensing procedures would only apply from the country on whose soil the weapons or components are manufactured and exported, not under export rules of every collaborating member – the process in place before the Agreement was established.

The Agreement is a far cry from another European agreement on arms transfers, which was signed two years before – the *EU Code of Conduct on Arms Exports.* This Code recognizes the need for 'high common standards which should be regarded as the minimum for the management, and restraint of, conventional arms transfers by all Member States.'[8] For more on the EU Code of Conduct, see chapter 8.

Blurring the boundaries: licensed production

In *The Arms Industry*, Chris Wrigley notes: 'The simple concept of an arms company disappears into a labyrinth of licensed production, joint ventures, conglomerates, strategic partnerships, and Co-operative Armament Programs. The concept of arms trade becomes equally elusive. When weapons 'systems' may be designed in one country, manufactured piecemeal in several others and sold both to the collaborating states and to others, what is an export and who is the exporter? Indeed, what are arms, when a harmless Land Rover vehicle may be sold or licensed to a semi-respectable government and turn up later, equipped with armor, radio and machine-guns, in the service of a distinctly disreputable one?'

As we are beginning to see, the arms trade has never really been about one arms company in one country selling a single weapons system to another country's government in exchange for a fat check. The arms trade is much more of a complex web, and campaigning against it is more complicated than at first appears.

One of the clearest examples of the complexity of arms deals, and a classic demonstration of how unscrupulous arms dealers, fixers and firms will gratuitously exploit loopholes in pursuit of a fast profit, is the problem of licensed production.

At its simplest, licensed production entails the vendor corporation supplying ready-to-assemble parts

Not just things that go 'bang'

A British anti-arms trade campaigner told me once that when he worked as an electrician for GEC, his department was responsible for testing some of the electronic components that would eventually drive the latest fighter planes. He knew this, but didn't really think about it. His job was just to test the components in a box.

This story illustrates a common misconception: that the arms trade is all about the buying and selling of things that go 'bang'. It is about planes like Hawk, Harrier and Tornado; it involves selling heat-seeking missiles, armed warheads and bombs; it is about armored tanks and submarines; and it is about guns, rifles, rocket launchers and grenades. But the trade in military *matériel* is also about components: the nuts and bolts, the metal panels and the plastic switches, the wheels and electronics that make the systems work. Otokar, a Turkish company, is licensed by the Rover car group to assemble their 4x4 Land Rover vehicle. The car parts are listed as civilian transfer from Rover in Britain, and therefore don't need an export license.

In 1994, Otokar started producing the Scorpion counter-insurgency vehicle, of which 70 to 80 per cent is comprised of Land Rover parts. Machine guns have been bolted onto the Scorpions, creating a terrifying armored vehicle, which has been used to perpetrate human rights with instructions, like a child's modeling kit, to another country which puts it together. At the other end of the scale, the vendor will supply technology and expertise – even expert engineers – and the buying country manufactures the system from scratch.

Licensed production is of concern because it blurs the boundaries of export licensing procedures. When a weapons system is exported from most states, the manufacturer has to apply for permission (an export license) to export it to another country. Permission is granted according to whatever criteria the exporting country might set. Campaigners are forever lobbying to have the criteria tightened up, for criteria to be adhered to, to prevent arms exports to regions of tension or human rights abuse, or to developing nations already plunged into debt.

But many countries have no specific export licensing procedures for equipment and technology intended for licensed production. A gaping hole is left

---

abuses by the Turkish military, and has also been sold on from Turkey to Algeria and Pakistan.

Part of the industry is about the trade in information and technology – weapons design, knowledge and engineering skill. In some licensed production deals, no hardware is exchanged at all – merely the license to produce a weapons system, and the instruction manual on how to build and use it.

Prison and policing equipment – riot shields, handguns, CS gas, truncheons, water cannon, armored vehicles – are also part of the arms business. Between 1980 and 1993, the US authorized licenses worth $5 million under the export category OA82, which includes thumb cuffs, leg irons, shackles, handcuffs and other police equipment. The US is also one of the world's largest innovators in, and exporters of, chemical crowd control equipment – pepper spray, tear gas and similar.

As if all this were not enough, the despicable trade includes, alarmingly, the buying and selling of sheer human might – it is about mercenaries, or private armies. Whether the hiring of private armies is to supplement a country's armed forces or fight off rebels, to defend a lucrative diamond mine, or to overthrow a dictator, it is still part of the dirty business. ■

in the ability to control arms exports.

In the same way, the export of technology, expertise and information can be more dangerous than exporting the system itself. Firstly, there can be no guarantee that the purchasing company won't continue to produce its own brand of the product, long after its original contract with the designing company has expired.

British firm, GKN Defence, set up a licensed production agreement with a company in the Philippines to produce Simba armored personnel carriers. A total of 150 vehicles were ordered. The company started with the assembly of kits, progressed to importing some parts and manufacturing others, and finished up producing whole vehicles that had nothing to do with the original contract.

Secondly, once a country is manufacturing its own arms there can be few restrictions on them selling on those arms, at a profit, to countries which would not have received an export license from the country where the system was originally designed.

Heckler & Koch (H&K), a small German arms company which is a subsidiary of BAE Systems, has licensed the production of its rifles to 14 countries, including Turkey, Burma and Pakistan. Turkish arms firm, MKEK, has been producing H&K weapons under license since the 1970s. Reportedly, 500 H&K submachine guns were shipped to Indonesia in September 1999, during a British arms embargo on the country for those kinds of weapons. Licensed production meant that arms, designed and overseen by a British-owned company, went to a country that Britain was currently refusing to arm. For more on licensed production, brokering and off-set deals, see chapter 6.

The global small arms market

Small arms require a special mention in any assessment of the global trade in armaments, simply because they are so prolific, the trade in them is so difficult to

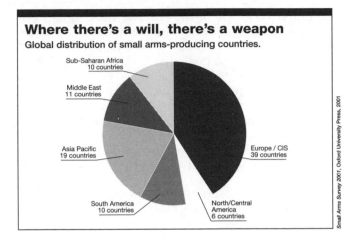

Where there's a will, there's a weapon

Global distribution of small arms-producing countries.

Sub-Saharan Africa
10 countries

Middle East
11 countries

Asia Pacific
19 countries

South America
10 countries

North/Central
America
6 countries

Europe / CIS
39 countries

Small Arms Survey 2001, Oxford University Press, 2001

control and the devastation caused by them is so severe.

Taking the definition of the UN panel of government experts on small arms, the category includes all of the following military, police and domestic weapons: revolvers and self-loading pistols, rifles and carbines, assault rifles, sub-machine guns and light machine guns, heavy machine guns, hand-held under-barrel and mounted grenade launchers, portable anti-tank and anti-aircraft guns, recoilless rifles, portable launchers of anti-tank and anti-aircraft systems, and mortars of less than 100 mm caliber.[9]

So there are plenty of them, and they are everywhere. They are used by police and security patrols, by national armies and by guerrilla and revolutionary groups, they are carried by civilians legally in a number of countries, for sport in many more, and illegally in every country. They feature in practically every armed conflict between nation-states, in internal and civil wars, in gang fighting and as status symbols.

They are so prolific because they are small and relatively cheap, easy to pass on, smuggle, hide, steal, capture from an enemy or buy over the counter. But they are also ubiquitous because of the sheer numbers they are produced in: millions of them, every day, all over the world. It is a myth that the trade in small arms is only one of recycling second- and third-hand weapons. New production merely creates more second- and third-hand guns. In 1999, 45 different countries reported to the UN that firearms, components and ammunition were legally produced in their territories for domestic or export markets. Many more countries didn't respond to the requests for information.[10]

The main producers of these little killers are China, Russia and the US. Another 20 or so countries, mainly in Europe and Asia, produce most of the rest of the world's supply. A further 29 countries produce nominal quantities mainly to meet their domestic requirements, or are currently unassessed.[11]

The nature of small arms, and the nature of the traffic in them – legal, illegal, underground market, civilian, smuggled, home-made – means there can

---

Small arms – huge impact

Forecast International, a commercial market-analysis company, makes the following estimates about the proliferation of small arms manufacture in their *Ordnance and Munitions Forecast*, published in October 2000:

- More than 43 million military-style small arms of all types were produced outside the US, between 1980 and 1999.
- More than 1.4 million military-style small arms of all types were produced for the US armed forced between 1970 and 1999.
- 37,000 small arms were produced for the US armed forces during 2000.

According to the US Bureau of Alcohol, Firearms and Tobacco (BAFT), around 4.37 million firearms are produced in the US every year. According to the *Small Arms Survey 2001*, it is estimated that at least 347 million small arms were produced worldwide between 1945 and 2000. ■

All figures quoted here are from *Small Arms Survey 2001: Profiling the Problem*, Oxford University Press, 2001.

never be accurate data on which countries have the most of them. Even if there were, accurate figures for exactly which of these were legal, illegal, military or civilian would be impossible to determine.

'The total number and global distribution of small arms remains one of the greatest enigmas in the field of international peace and security', says the *Small Arms Survey*.[12]

The *Survey* is a project of the Graduate Institute of International Studies in Geneva, which has attempted to profile and estimate the proliferation of firearms (hand-held guns and rifles, rather than hand-held missile launchers and the like), based on rough estimates and incomplete reporting by countries.

Their research estimates that there are at least 550 million legally-held firearms in the world today – at least one gun for every 11 of the world's people. Over half of all of these are privately owned. The group was unable, not surprisingly, to estimate the number of illegally-held arms in the world.

1 *The Arms Industry*, Chris Wrigley, Campaign Against Arms Trade, March 2001. **2** *SIPRI Yearbook 2001,* Stockholm International Peace Research Institute. **3** 'Confronting the military-corporate complex', Stephen Staples, Hague Appeal for Peace, 12.5.99. **4** *SIPRI Yearbook 2001,* Stockholm International Peace Research Institute. **5** *Conventional Arms Transfers to Developing Nations, 1993-2000,* Richard Grimmett, Congressional Research Service Report, August 2001. **6** *The Arms Industry*, Chris Wrigley, Campaign Against Arms Trade, March 2001. **7** *The expansion of NATO*, Campaign Against Arms Trade, March 1999. **8** *The EU Code of Conduct on Arms Exports,* 3rd preambular paragraph. **9** *Report of the Panel of Governmental Experts on Small Arms,* United Nations document A/52/298, 27 August 1997. **10** *International Study on Firearm Regulation (1999),* United Nations. **11** *Small Arms Survey 2001: Profiling the Problem,* Oxford University Press, 2001. **12** *Small Arms Survey 2001: Profiling the Problem,* Oxford University Press, 2001.

2 Impact on conflicts

A world at war... The nature of conflict, the boomerang effect, small arms and combat... Examples of hostilities and their military quartermasters.

THE 20TH CENTURY was the most violent one in human history. Not only did it witness two world wars, and 30 years of major arms-fuelled tension between the world's superpowers, it also featured hundreds of localized conflicts, armed border disputes, civil wars, military coups and counter coups, revolutionary struggles and armed invasions.

According to the *Armed Conflicts Report 2000* and the *State of the World Report 1999*, there were 40 armed conflicts underway in 36 different countries as the 21st century was born. Even in the short time since the millennium, the world has witnessed a new 'war on terror' waged by the US and its allies against Afghanistan, with the threat of extension to Somalia, and the possibility of intensified attacks on Iraq.

Earth is a planet at war, and to a large extent this is a consequence of the legal and illicit sale of arms. In crude but plain terms, without weaponry, combat would be more limited in scale.

In most conflict zones in the world, war is a way of life. Waging war is a means of generating money, exerting political power, and providing employment. In some areas of the developing world, children grow up knowing nothing else but bloodshed, dead, injured or maimed relatives, the daily risk of landmines; even bearing arms themselves. If they survive long enough to procreate, their own children will know only the same.

War today

Despite tension between India and Pakistan, the future stability of the world is probably now less at risk from an all-out nuclear catastrophe – as was thought during the Cold War era – than from a slow, insidious, systematic proliferation of small wars and local strife in mainly smaller nations, many of them in Africa. In 1998, Africa suffered 11 major armed conflicts. It is now the most war-torn region in the world.

Those small wars are created and sustained in a constant battle to control territory, plunder resources and wield power. William Hartung, of the World Policy Institute, illustrates the problem. When the current Liberian president Charles Taylor invaded Liberia on Christmas Eve in 1989, he did so with just 100 irregular soldiers, armed with AK-47 rifles. Within months they had seized mineral and timber resources and used the profits to purchase more light weapons: the first few turns in an ongoing vicious cycle.

According to Hartung: 'This pattern of war as plunder has been repeated with local variations in Sierra Leone, where the Liberian-backed Revolutionary United Front (RUF) has used diamond sales to fuel its campaign of terror; in Colombia, where government forces, right-wing paramilitaries and anti-government rebels have skimmed off profits, fees and bribes from the cocaine trade; in Angola, where UNITA rebel forces have raised billions of dollars through diamond sales and the Angolan Government has countered by stocking its arsenal with revenues drawn from its large offshore oil deposits.'[1]

The seizure or trafficking of drugs, diamonds and other valuable commodities produces profits for warring factions. Profits are spent not on peace, reconciliation or education, but on more weapons – bought on the illicit market, and through more 'legitimate' channels.

The weapons suppliers to the perpetrators of the 1994 genocide in Rwanda included brokers and shippers in Britain, South Africa and France, working with collaborators in Albania, Belgium, Bulgaria, Egypt, Italy, the Seychelles and the former Zaire (now DR

Congo/DRC). Arms and military training are also supplied to warring or revolutionary factions, both openly and secretly, by Western nations to serve their own political ambitions. See 'The boomerang effect' further on.

Bigger picture

But the arms trade also has a role in sustaining larger, more 'official' tensions and conflicts between states. The deadly dealing increases strains and thereby fuels wars between established nations.

Here are some examples. From 1989 to 1998, the US provided over $227 million in weapons and training to African military forces. Of this, over $111 million went to governments that have been directly or indirectly involved in the war in the Democratic Republic of Congo (DRC): Angola, Burundi, Chad, Namibia, Rwanda, Sudan, Uganda and Zimbabwe.

Planet earth is a world at war

Below are some of the countries currently involved in armed conflict.

Russia

UK

Yugoslavia
Turkey
Israel
US
Palestine
Algeria   Iraq Afghanistan
Pakistan

Sudan   Burma
India

Liberia Nigeria Somalia Sri Lanka Philippines
Colombia   Congo Uganda
DR Congo Kenya   Indonesia
Burundi

Angola

Peace Pledge Union www.ppu.org.uk

The big seven arms-selling countries in the world – the US, France, Germany, Britain, Russia, China and Italy have all sold arms to states currently involved in conflict including Sri Lanka, Indonesia, Israel, China, Taiwan, India and Pakistan. And they usually show off their deadly wares at arms fairs.

The problem of arms fairs

Fairs and exhibitions are the most outward manifestation of the tendency of the arms trade to supply countries currently at war or in conflict with each other. Every year countries shop at exhibitions taking place all over the world. Arms companies show their very best weaponry – their most modern killing and 'defense' equipment.

The deals do take place at the fairs themselves, but these are also meeting and networking places – where delegates can begin relationships with the companies, later going on to discuss, in privacy, their military needs and what is available.

Countries hosting arms fairs often argue that they would not necessarily sell *matériel* to every country that attends, but this is a bluff. Every delegate invited to an arms fair is a potential customer, not just for the host nation, but of every corporate exhibitor.

Anti-arms trade campaigners work hard to expose these exhibitions for what they really are – the hub of the international arms trade. British activists protested in their thousands outside the Defence Systems Equipment International (DSEi) arms fair in London in 2001 (see box p 33). They were cordoned off and harassed by police. The area they were given to protest in was hidden away from where the delegates and dealers arrived, and from the general public. A number of direct activists were arrested for attempting to stop delegates from reaching the fair.

The boomerang effect

A week before the attacks on America, political humorist

Art Buchwald asked, 'How can we work for peace when we are preparing so many countries for war?'

One of the most frequent arguments that politicians and arms company executives use to justify their lethal industry is that weapons help to create stability in the world. Countries have a right to defend themselves from attack. When the West is covertly, or openly, supplying arms to rebel and revolutionary movements that accord with their interests, they argue that oppressed people have a right to attempt to overthrow their oppressor and install democracy.

But it is an old saying that your friend today may become your enemy in the future, and in no field is this truer than in the world of weaponry. We in the West may happily arm a country today, but we cannot predict whether, at some time in the future, we may be facing those very same munitions in a conflict with that country – as happened for example with the Malvinas/Falklands war against Argentina when British forces faced 'friendly' French Exocet missiles.

During the Soviet occupation of Afghanistan, the US and Europe (including Britain) shipped tons of arms to rebels fighting the Soviets. An estimated 250 to 350 surface-to-air missile launchers (Britain supplied Blowpipe, the US supplied Stinger) were used in the 1980s Afghan conflict. Many of the same Mujahedin-backed rebels who took the Afghan capital in 1996 are known today as the Taliban. At the end of 2001, the US and Britain were at war with them, and their estimated remaining 100 Stingers, as part of the 'war against terrorism'.

During the 1980s, the US transferred billions of tons of light weaponry to right-wing rebels in Central America, South Asia and Southern Africa. These covert arms sales were viewed as a legitimate expression of US interests – the battle against Communism. But the sales have boomeranged.

'[They] have since served as the seedbed for the proliferation of small arms to a motley crew of terrorists, separatists, and militia leaders, and fuelled conflicts

from Kashmir and Tajikistan, to the Democratic
Republic of Congo,' as the World Policy Institute's
William Hartung notes. 'Small arms almost always out-
last the political relationships that existed between the
original supplier and recipient, and one needs look no
farther than the anti-US activities of Osama bin Laden
and his network of the former Afghan freedom fighters
to see how covert arms sales can come back to haunt
the supplier nations.'[2]

Other places where US troops faced adversaries
armed with US military hardware include Panama,
Iraq, Somalia and Haiti.

Military training

Military training is an aspect of the industry often over-
looked by campaigners and politicians working towards
arms control. Yet the provision of training to foreign
armies, or warring factions, is commonplace and was

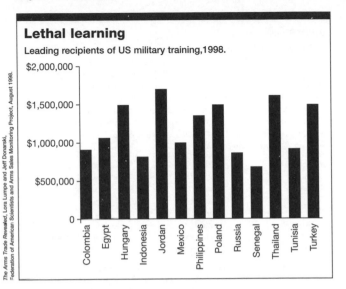

Lethal learning

Leading recipients of US military training, 1998.

The Arms Trade Revealed, Lora Lumpe and Jeff Donarski, Federation of American Scientists and Arms Sales Monitoring Project, August 1998.

clearly illustrated with the allied forces' training and assistance given to the Afghan United Front forces during their reclaiming of Afghanistan at the end of 2001.

Just as with the hardware, military training is used by governments to further their strategic and political objectives, as well as being a tool in international relations. But like arms sales, military training of foreign fighters can also bounce back.

Since the US armed forces are among the most highly trained and best financially supported in the world, it is no surprise that the US is a major provider of military training. Here's an example.

Towards the end of his presidency, Bill Clinton took a special interest in Africa. His proposed 'new partnership' was not to supply aid or help build civil society as was hoped, but apparently to establish a wide program of troop training. In 1998, the US provided $45.8 million in international military education training (IMET) for over 400 African soldiers.

Under the Pentagon's Joint Combined Exchange

Training (JCET) program, US Special Forces have trained military personnel from at least 34 of Africa's 53 nations. That includes troops fighting on both sides of the DRC's 'civil' war – from Rwanda and Uganda (supporting the rebels) to Zimbabwe and Namibia (supporting DRC's Kabila regime).

When Rwandan soldiers invaded DR Congo (then called Zaire) in 1996, attacking refugees and massacring civilians, the US was forced to defend its training of Rwandan troops. *The Washington Post* revealed that the troops had received combat training from the US, as well as human rights training.

Conflict and small arms

As described above, most modern wars do not pit one nation state against another, and rarely even one government against an insurgent or militia movement. The majority of today's wars are complex and multi-faceted, waged by rebel groups, warlords, gangs and governments. The warring factions know little of, or care little about, the established rules of war – they engage in calculated terror campaigns, revenge killings and assassinations. Civilians are considered a legitimate target.

These wars are not fought with fighter planes and long-range missiles, or even with tanks and rocket-launchers. They are fought with hand-held guns, rifles and pistols.

'The ready availability of small arms,' notes Hartung, 'makes these conflicts far more likely to occur, far more deadly once they start, and far more difficult to resolve once the death tolls mount and the urge for revenge takes hold.'[3]

Light weapons were the only armaments used in most major conflicts fought worldwide during the 1990s. They have been linked to the vast increase in civilian deaths generated in today's wars – an estimated 80 per cent, compared with only five per cent at the beginning of the 20th century.

Dirty dozen

The main suppliers of small arms include the same dozen governments that dominate the trade. The main government suppliers include the US, Russia, China, France and Britain, along with Belgium, Bulgaria, Germany, Israel, Italy and South Africa. Innumerable independent arms dealers, criminals, brokers and middlemen control the illicit trade.

Some governments and campaigners draw a distinction between legally transferred small arms, and the illegal trade. The vast majority of small arms which infest southern Africa were originally supplied 'legitimately' by the USSR to 'liberation movements' there. Ukraine, Belarus and Bulgaria remain large suppliers to the region.

Worldwide, the 'legal' trade makes up by far the majority of small arms sales. Transfers from established companies, within established nations, make up nearly 90 per cent of the total annual value of the trade. The annual legal global trade in small arms and light weapons is estimated at $4-6 billion. This represents transfers of arms to police services, military and security forces as well as to the domestic and sporting market.

It will be for the reader to draw their own moral boundaries between the legal and illicit market, but it is worth pointing out that without the legal trade in weapons, the illegal trade would not exist. It can be argued that all legal small arms transfers should be of concern to campaigners for a number of reasons.

As with the transfer of tanks, planes and bombs, the trade in light weapons between governments is a problem if these are used to perpetrate human rights abuses.

Turkey is a clear example. The now British-owned company Heckler & Koch (H&K) has signed a licensed production deal to supply upwards of 600,000 assault rifles to the Turkish army with the blessing of the British Government. Yet the Turkish military has been implicated in repressive human rights abuses against the Kurdish people in the south of the country, where Kurds are routinely arrested for celebrating their national heritage, or even for speaking their own language.

The Philippines receives substantial legal small arms transfers from the US and Europe, Canada and South Africa, yet it is already saturated with light weapons and is notorious as an arms-trafficking hub. Thailand and Singapore are in a similar position, with large numbers transferred to them in 2000.

Another aspect is that when armed forces buy new weapons, their older ones often cascade into the semi-legal (gray) trade or into the illegal trade. (The US 'right to bear arms' market for domestic weapons is the main source of illegal weapon ownership there). As more weapons clatter onto the market, whether legal or illegal, the cheaper they become – and so the more readily available to rebel fighters, civilians and even children.

Likewise, legally transferred weapons find their way onto the illegal market through other means: corrupt officials, the looting of arms stockpiles and poor security measures.

Murky markets

The semi-legal (gray) and black markets in light arms are together worth an estimated $1 billion annually.[4] Given their relatively small extent – compared to the legal trade in arms – the gray and black markets have received disproportionate concern from politicians and campaigners alike. There is no doubt that it is the illegal arms market that is the driving force behind civil conflicts, corruption, crime and random violence, but as described above, they really owe their strength to the legal trade.

The 'gray' market refers to transfers of light weapons that are only on the edge of legality. It encompasses those supplied covertly to rebel forces by governments with an interest in their success, or transfers struck via arms brokers who exploit loopholes in arms control legislation to make sales of second-hand weapons stockpiled from finished conflicts on the other side of the world.

The illegal trade is easier to define, but is much harder to quantify, by its very nature. Black market transfers are made in clear violation of national and international laws, without permission or consent from governments.

The small arms market, with its legal, gray and black constituents is the murkiest market of all: this is precisely what makes it so hard to monitor, control and ultimately attempt to abolish. Below are some examples.

Sierra Leone – This small African nation has hosted one of the most brutal small-arms driven conflicts in modern times, which has included child soldiers. The munitions trade is driven by the desire of rebel movements to control and benefit from the country's diamond mines. The Revolutionary United Front (RUF) has been at the forefront of the troubles, and has committed some of the worst human rights abuses in the ongoing conflict.

RUF sources for firearms, paid for by diamonds, include Liberia, Libya, Burkina Faso, Côte d'Ivoire, Slovakia and Ukraine. The weapons come by circuitous routes and Western companies and dealers have been implicated in the transfers. There have even been reports of sales of weapons by UN troops. In May 2000, a journalist reported having viewed depots of confiscated arms in Sierra Leone. He stated that there were over 12,000 small arms, mainly of Ukrainian, Iranian and Belgian origin and 389,877 rounds of ammunition.

The Balkans – Ethnic wars throughout the 1990s created a high demand for small arms. One of the main sources was the civilian looting of Albanian military depots, where more than 600,000 weapons were stolen. More than 500,000 remain in civilian hands. The Kosovo Liberation Army (KLA) and its organized crime networks have been responsible for considerable arms trafficking. Germany, Austria and Switzerland (countries with large Kosovar populations) have been a source for large numbers of small arms smuggled by the KLA.

It has now been reported that Bosnia-Herzegovina have become a source for surplus arms since the ceasefire in the Balkans. Croatian officials stopped a shipment of portable rocket launchers, assault rifles, ammunition and explosives in July 2000, and suspected that the arms came from Bosnia-Herzegovina. After investigations, they concluded the weapons had been bound for the Northern Ireland terror group, the Real IRA.

War in the Congo

The ongoing bloody conflict in the Democratic Republic of Congo (DRC), formerly Zaire, has been called Africa's 'first world war'.

In 1965 Mobutu Sese Seko became president of Zaire with the backing of the US Central Intelligence Agency (CIA), who needed a strategic friend in Africa. Mobutu quickly became one of the continent's most brutal dictators, but was nevertheless supported by the US in weapons sales and military training. Even after the Cold War, the United States continued to supply military support to the Mobutu regime. In 1991, more than $4.5 million of military equipment was delivered to Zaire.

In 1996 and 1997, Laurent Kabila and his Alliance of Democratic Forces fought running battles with the Mobutu dictatorship, eventually ousting the despot. The US immediately offered the Kabila regime military training, even as the new president suspended human rights and banned opposition political parties. On 2 August 1998, DR Congo's current brutal conflict began, with nine African nations siding with either the

Mobutu faction or Kabila regime in a fight for DR Congo's rich mineral and diamond resources.

Foreign troops from Rwanda, Uganda, Burundi, Angola, Namibia, Sudan, Chad and Zimbabwe have all been drawn into the fight, along with irregular and guerrilla movements from surrounding African states. US, Britain, China, Russia, South Africa and other weapons-selling giants have gathered like vultures, gladly supplying the factions with weapons of death. Even after six of the governments involved were drawn together to sign the Lusaka peace accords in July 2000, the battling continues, supported by Western countries and their arms companies.

Despite not sharing a border with the DRC, Robert Mugabe's Zimbabwe has played a major part in the tensions since the mid-1990s in support of the Kabila regime. It is widely known that Zimbabwe sent a steady supply of North Korean weapons to Kabila's rebels before they came to power. In 2000, Zimbabwe had an estimated 13,000 troops fighting in the DR Congo. The Government then estimated its involvement in the DRC cost $3 million a month – though leaked documents

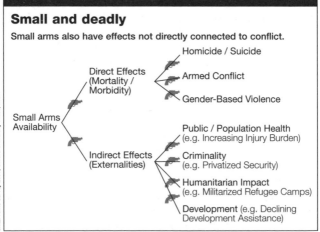

Small and deadly

Small arms also have effects not directly connected to conflict.

- Small Arms Availability
  - Direct Effects (Mortality / Morbidity)
    - Homicide / Suicide
    - Armed Conflict
    - Gender-Based Violence
  - Indirect Effects (Externalities)
    - Public / Population Health (e.g. Increasing Injury Burden)
    - Criminality (e.g. Privatized Security)
    - Humanitarian Impact (e.g. Militarized Refugee Camps)
    - Development (e.g. Declining Development Assistance)

Small Arms Survey 2001, Oxford University Press, 2001.

have put the figure closer to $27 million, a price the country can ill afford with unemployment at more than 50 per cent, huge debts and massive inflation.

Britain has been a good friend to Zimbabwe in terms of arms sales, continuing to supply even after a June 1999 call by the Presidency of the European Union (EU) for states to observe a 'rigorous application' of the EU Code of Conduct on arms sales regarding the region.

In February 2000, the British *Guardian* newspaper revealed that the Prime Minister, Tony Blair, had pushed through licenses for Hawk fighter jet spare parts to Zimbabwe even though there was evidence that Hawks had been used in the Congo conflict. Only three months later was Robin Cook, the embattled 'ethical foreign policy' British Foreign Secretary, able to announce a full arms embargo on the country – after Zimbabwean white farmers had been attacked by Mugabe supporters. But by that time, many of the Hawk parts had already been exported.

India and Pakistan

In early 2002, the UK's Tony Blair, with the support of US President George W Bush, was visiting India and Pakistan supposedly to 'cool tensions' between the historic enemies, who were again on the brink of war over the disputed Kashmir territory. But it very soon emerged that he spent much of his time in both countries pushing British arms, especially encouraging India to finally sign a BAE Systems contract to receive 60 Hawk fighter jets, worth $1.45 billion. At the time of writing, that deal still hadn't been secured.

Battles over strips of land are not new in international relations, but the India-Pakistan conflict is all the more alarming because both have nuclear weapons.

India, already by far the dominant in terms of military might, is spending $95 billion over the next 15 years modernizing its arsenal. Russia is the principal supplier and is lined up to supply $10 billion worth of arms over the next decade, including fighter planes, air defenses and submarines. India is also developing a close relationship with Israel, whose own arms industry has high-tech weaponry to offer.[5]

Pakistan is also seeking to modernize, choosing China as its main military partner, recently receiving the first of 50 Chinese F-7MG fighters. In addition, Pakistan obtains sophisticated weaponry from France, including aircraft and submarines, battle tanks from the Ukraine, and Turkish-built armored cars made from British-supplied Land Rover parts.

Both India and Pakistan were invited to shop for arms at an exhibition in London on 11 September, the day of the terrorist attacks on the World Trade Center and the Pentagon. Those attacks also radically changed Washington's attitude to supplying arms to India and Pakistan. Just one month later, the US removed arms and military sanctions on the countries (originally levied because of the nuclear issue), in exchange of support in its war against terrorism.

Israel

In January 2002, Israeli soldiers stopped and commandeered a cargo ship in the Red Sea. On board were found thousands of tons of illegally sold small arms, including rifles, missile launchers and mortars. Prime Minister Ariel Sharon declaimed this as an arms shipment to Islamic terrorists in the Gaza Strip, and used it as further justification to reject peace accords with the Palestinian movement.

Almost every day, new reports of street battles, atrocities and bombings emerge from the occupied territories. While the Palestinians receive most of their arms on the black market from the supportive Muslim Middle East, Israel is generously backed by the West. Wherever nations stand on the territory and the legitimacy of an independent Palestinian state, the supply of weapons, whether covertly or 'legally' does little to ease the tensions.

On 3 October 2000, the Clinton administration in the US signed a deal to supply the largest purchase in a decade of military helicopters by the Israeli Defense Force (IDF), and spare parts for Apache helicopters were also supplied. US marines carried out joint exercises with the IDF one month earlier.

Apaches with rockets were used on 4 October 2000 to attack an apartment complex in Palestinian Netzarim. A few weeks later, the local Palestinian leader Hussein Abayat and two women civilians were killed by a missile launched from an Apache.

According to US commentator, Noam Chomsky, officials told journalists: 'US weapons sales do not carry a stipulation that the weapons can't be used against civilians. We cannot second-guess an Israeli commander who calls in helicopter gunships.'[6]

British arms export licenses granted to Israel during 2000 included licenses categorized under arms and automatic weapons; aircraft and aircraft related goods including combat aircraft; and imaging or countermeasure equipment.

Sri Lanka's internal war

Sri Lanka is a classic example of an internal conflict exacerbated by Western arms supplies.

For many years a civil war has raged in the tiny country between the government in Colombo and the Liberation Tigers of Tamil Elam (LTTE, or Tamil Tigers), who wished to establish a separate Tamil-speaking state in the north and east of the island. Between 1983 and 1998, over 20,000 people were killed; several hundred in a brutal battle in September 1998.

The Sri Lankan military stood at around 160,000 in 1997. According to the Campaign Against Arms Trade (CAAT), it was 'a monster which is now itself a major political force and, in the opinion of many observers, a threat to Sri Lanka's democracy. Even if the Government was ready to compromise with the LTTE, the army would probably not allow them to do so.'[7]

Impact on conflicts

The army has some old Soviet tanks, bought from the Czech republic in 1996, and a variety of lighter armored vehicles, some built in Britain. It sports a few elderly US fighters and some more modern Israeli planes, plus US and Russian attack helicopters.

The Tigers are equipped almost entirely with light weapons, including shoulder-held missiles, which have destroyed a number of government aircraft. Much of their arsenal has been captured from government sources, but their weapons-purchasing power on the black market is strong, given Tamil diaspora support of some $1.87 million a month.

Both sides in the conflict have been criticized for terrible human rights abuses. The Tigers are brutal and regardless fighters. The Sri Lankan response has been the attempted crushing of Tamil civilians. Its ultimate intention has been the destruction of opposition forces by virtually any means.

Yet the Sri Lankan Government still receives weapons exports from Western states. In 1997-8, the first year of the Labour Government in Britain which came into power championing an 'ethical foreign policy', 67 licenses were granted for the sale of military equipment to Sri Lanka.

1,2,3 'The New Business of War: Small Arms and the Proliferation of Conflict', William Hartung, in *Ethics and International Affairs*, Carnegie Council on Ethics and International Affairs. **4** Much of the information here is taken directly from *Small Arms Survey 2001: Profiling the Problem*, Oxford University Press, 2001. **5** *India and Pakistan: The Military Balance*, BBC News Online, 31 December 2001. **6** 'Fuelling the conflict', Noam Chomsky, *CAAT News*, October/November 2001, Campaign Against Arms Trade. **7** *The supply of military equipment to Sri Lanka*, Campaign Against Arms Trade, November 1998.

3 Impact on human rights

How weapons sales help perpetuate human rights abuses... and give political support to the countries that perpetrate them... The trade in torture, policing and surveillance equipment... The problem of refugees.

'No security assistance may be provided to any country the government of which engages in a consistent pattern of gross violations of internationally recognized human rights.'

Section 502B, US Foreign Assistance Act.

'The President shall consider the following criteria... The government of the country... was chosen by and permits free and fair elections... respects human rights... does not persistently engage in gross violations of internationally recognized human rights, including extra-judicial or arbitrary executions, disappearances, torture or severe mistreatment, prolonged arbitrary imprisonment...'

US International Arms Sales Code of Conduct Act 1999.

'Member States will not issue an export license if there is a clear risk that the proposed export might be used for internal repression... [including] torture and other cruel, inhuman and degrading treatment or punishment, summary or arbitrary executions, disappearances, arbitrary detentions and other major violations of human rights.'

EU Code of Conduct for Arms Exports 1998

DESPITE THE IMPRESSIVE rhetoric above, human rights have not been a major barrier to weapons sales at any time in history. The world's worst dictators, despots, human rights abusers and anti-democratic regimes have been the customers of all of the major arms supplying countries in the world – and continue to be so. Campaigners have been working for years to prevent arms sales to human rights abusing states as a matter of urgency.

Human rights abuse takes many forms, and is not easily definable or strictly delimited. It ranges from banning certain languages to extra-judicial killings; from physical torture to widespread state-sponsored repression of a particular race or minority. It might include the banning of teaching of a particular philosophy, outlook or worldview. It could include an autocratic or dictatorial political system, which does not allow free elections and bans alternative political parties and visions.

Whatever the definition, the arms trade perpetuates, worsens and legitimizes the systematic abuse of human rights all over the world.

The supply of equipment that can be used to carry out human rights abuses, such as torture equipment, chemicals, restraint equipment and military hardware, supports the abuse because it provides the oppressor with the tools to carry out his actions. And those actions need not be directly connected to the

United Nations Universal Declaration of Human Rights

Article 2

Everyone is entitled to all the rights and freedoms set forth in this Declaration, without distinction of any kind, such as race, color, sex, language, religion, political or other opinion, national or social origin, property, birth or other status.

Article 5

No one shall be subjected to torture or to cruel, inhuman or degrading treatment or punishment.

Article 9

No one shall be subjected to arbitrary arrest, detention or exile.

Article 10

Everyone is entitled in full equality to a fair and public hearing by an independent and impartial tribunal, in the determination of his/her rights and obligations and of any criminal charge against him/her.

The full text can be found at: www.un.org/overview/rights

equipment in question. A military vehicle, which carries soldiers and their flame-throwers to burn down a refugee camp, is as involved in the abuse as the weapons and soldiers themselves.

In addition, arms sales always carry with them a political value. Whatever arms are being supplied to a regime, whether or not they are used in human rights abuses, they confer political and moral legitimacy to the state to which they are being sold. Whether the Hawk aircraft, supplied by Britain to Indonesia, were used over East Timor or not is irrelevant in terms of whether their sale helped to confer legitimacy to the murderous Suharto regime.

Western democracies like to argue that they use arms sales as bartering chips in negotiations with countries with repressive human rights records, in order to urge them to clean up their act. History has shown this argument to be false.

An example, which would be amusing if it wasn't so shocking, is when Chinese president Jiang Zemin visited London, England, in October 1999. The UK Government refused to publicly raise China's terrible human rights record with the President. According to Amnesty International, 'Hundreds of followers of "heretical" religious or spiritual movements were arrested and reportedly tortured, [including] Falun Gong followers...and hundreds of Buddhist nuns and monks in Tibet. Ethnic Uighurs labelled as "separatists" or "terrorists" were executed mostly after secret or summary trials where convictions were based on confessions extracted under torture.'[1]

At Zemin's UK visit, press and protesters were physically hidden by police vans in order to avoid causing offense to the Chinese delegation. Rather than exporting good human rights practice to China, Britain apparently imported Chinese values of heavy-handed policing, curbed media and intolerance of political dissent.

According to the Center for International Policy,

during the fiscal year 1998 around 54 per cent of US arms transfers to the developing world went to undemocratic regimes. Between 1991 and 1994, 85 per cent of all US arms transfers were to undemocratic states.[2]

According to one calculation by William Hartung of the World Policy Institute, during the 1999 fiscal year, the US delivered roughly $6.8 billion in armaments to nations which violate the basic standards set out in the US's own International Code of Conduct on Arms Sales.[3]

The trade in torture

Torture is prohibited in all circumstances by international law[4]. Torture and inhuman treatment, ill-treatment and degrading practices are the trademarks of repressive states – many of which are supplied with their torture weapons, or political support, by countries which also sell them arms.

Companies and individuals all over the world are involved in supplying devices and expertise, even training, in torture. In some terrible cases, equipment specifically designed for torture is supplied. In others, devices and material that can easily be used for torture are supplied, without hesitation, to police and security forces well known for their techniques in inflicting pain and degrading treatment using whatever tools they can obtain.

Torture equipment and devices such as police batons and handcuffs that can easily be used for torture are shipped under the auspices of arms and are regarded as legitimate goods for sale and purchase by many governments. There are also huge black and 'gray' markets in torture equipment – an illegal market in specially designed weapons, as well as networks of brokers, shippers and fixers ready to exploit loopholes and try legal boundaries in order to profit from equipment sales.

Restraint equipment

Handcuffs, leg cuffs, shackles and restraint belts are

Tools of torture

Below are the main countries whose manufacturers produce and sell torture stun weapons

Country	Number of manufacturers distributors, suppliers or brokers of stun weapons known to AI*		Country	Number of manufacturers distributors, suppliers or brokers of stun weapons known to AI*	
	1998-2000	1990-97		1998-2000	1990-97
Argentina		1	Luxembourg		1
Austria	1		Macedonia	1	
Belgium		1	Mexico	2	4
Brazil	3	1	Philippines	1	
Canada	1	1	Poland	5	
China	9	5	Romania	1	
Czech Rep.	1		Russia	3	1
France	6	8	Saudi Arabia		1
Germany	11	11	South Korea	8	4
Hungary		1	South Africa	7	1
Indonesia	1	1	Spain	1	
Israel	6	2	Taiwan	17	7
Japan		1	Turkey	1	1
Kuwait	1		UK		8
Lebanon	1		US	42	55
Lithuania	1				

* Amnesty International

Stopping the Torture Trade, Amnesty International, 2001.

used all over the world to inflict pain, suffering and degradation on prisoners. Of course it can be argued that some mechanical equipment, like handcuffs, does have legitimate uses – but in the hands of human rights abusers they can be used directly or indirectly to cause pain. Other devices, like restraint chairs and the rack, have little use except for torture.

Amnesty International (AI) has received countless reports of the ill use of US and UK-made restraining devices in Saudi Arabia.

AI has also received reports of misuse of restraint devices on children in Pakistan, prisoners in Thailand and political opponents in Yemen. The practice of *shabeh*, reportedly used in Israel, involves shackling a person in a painful and unnatural position for hours, while leaving little visible sign of damage on the body. In parts of the US it is still common for prisoners, including sick people and pregnant women, to be shackled by any combination of hand, waist, leg and ankle cuffs.

Several countries, including Britain and Latvia, have

Surveillance as repressive technology

'The surveillance trade is almost indistinguishable from the arms trade. More than 70 per cent of companies manufacturing and exporting surveillance technology also export arms, chemical weapons, or military hardware. Surveillance is a crucial element for the maintenance of any non-democratic infrastructure, and is an important activity in the pursuit of intelligence and political control. Many countries in transition to democracy also rely heavily on surveillance to satisfy the demands of police and military.' *Big Brother Incorporated*, Privacy International, 1995.

Arms and technology companies in Europe and North America have provided the surveillance infrastructure for the secret police and military authorities in repressive regimes including China, Indonesia, Nigeria, Angola, Rwanda and Guatemala.

Like armed vehicles, or the engines that keep bomber jets in the air, surveillance technology is part of the international arms trade that does not actually go 'bang' or directly cause suffering or death in repressive states, but it should still give cause for concern to campaigners.

The technology is used to track dissidents, human rights activists, journalists, trade unionists and anyone else who questions the authority of the state. It can also be used to co-ordinate brutal military attacks on innocent people.

One British computer firm provided the technological infrastructure to establish the South African passbook system, which was one of the foundations for the apartheid regime. British surveillance cameras were used during the Tiananmen Square crushing of pro-democracy demonstrators in Beijing, China, in 1989.

Companies supplying the Indonesian police and military with surveillance and targeting technology were from Britain, France and the US. Nigeria received its technology from Canada and Britain. China's surveillance equipment comes from Britain and the Netherlands. ■

Big Brother Incorporated, Privacy International, 1995.
The report can be viewed online at
www.privacy.org/pi/reports/big-bro/intro.html

begun moves to change legislation to prevent the use and export of certain types of restraint devices. (The British ban followed a public outcry, proving the positive effects of campaigning). While those restrictions are weak, they are at least something. Many other states, including the US, continue to use and export restraint devices widely. The absence of meaningful controls and monitoring procedures means both the legal and the illegal market continues unabated.

Chemicals and gases

The police use of chemicals and gases, especially in crowd control, has received much publicity with the growth of the anti-capitalist movements, and state attempts to disperse large protests.

During anti-capitalist protests in Genoa, Italy, in July 2001, I experienced their effects for myself. During a peaceful march down a narrow street towards the city center, where G8 leaders (from the world's richest nations) were meeting, a crowd of about 5,000 people was confronted by Italian military police who fired tear-gas canisters into the center of the protest. The gas rose up from the floor, stinging our eyes, throats and skin. The only option was to attempt to escape the searing smog, but there was nowhere to go.

Police and politicians argue that gas is used to disperse crowds in a tense situation, but it is also used as a tool of repression and intimidation.

In July 1997, Zambian police fired gas canisters into a building where a number of peaceful women and children demonstrators had sought refuge after an earlier tear gas attack.

A tear gas canister from this attack was passed to AI. It had been manufactured by Pains-Wessex, a UK firm. In July 2000, the British Government published its annual report on arms exports, revealing it was still supplying CS grenades and tear gas/irritant ammunition to Zambia.

After a similar incident in Kenya, where police fired

tear gas into a church and then beat anyone escaping, the British Government declared that it had rejected $2.1 million license applications for riot control equipment to the Kenyan police because of human rights concerns. But in June 1999, 2,000 peaceful demonstrators were violently dispersed by Kenyan police using tear gas, and water reportedly mixed with an irritant dye. The manufacturer of the gas was a French-based company. The absence of EU-wide or international regulations had allowed Kenya simply to find another seller.

Electro-shock equipment

AI reports that electro-shock devices have been used to torture or ill-treat people in prisons, detention centers or police stations in at least 76 countries, in every region of the world.

These are the ultimate weapon of choice for the torturer, who will cover the head or eyes of a victim and administer volts to the most sensitive parts of the body, including the mouth, buttocks and genitals, inflicting maximum pain without leaving permanent marks.

In September 1998, security forces in Phnom Penh, Cambodia, beat protesters, including Buddhist monks, with such weapons. More than 60 people needed hospital treatment. In the same year, electro-shock batons were used by the security forces in Kinshasa, in the DRC, against members of the main political opposition party. Other misuses of the technology, according to AI, have been reported in the US, Turkey, Saudi Arabia, South Africa, Egypt, China, Indonesia, Myanmar (Burma), Cyprus, Libya, Peru, Angola and North Korea.

Use of electro-shock batons, stun guns, shields and belts is frequent all over the world, including in democratic states who claim their legitimate use in police and prison control. The US, which was the leading developer of the technology, frequently uses stun belts.

Stun Tech Inc, the main US manufacturer, claims that its belts have been worn by prisoners on over 50,000 occasions. There are well over 1,000 belts in circulation in more than 100 American jurisdictions.

Virtually all companies that produce and market electro-shock devices claim they are medically safe and non-lethal if used properly. Not only have those claims been questioned, but in 2000 there were 130 companies across the world manufacturing these devices for all kinds of unscrupulous and murderous customers. Of these, significant manufacturers are located in the US, China, Taiwan and South Korea. There are few restrictions on their use or sale in China, Israel, South Africa, Russia, Taiwan or the US.

In European countries such as Belgium, Italy and Spain, according to the president of one French stun gun firm, 'they don't really know whether they're allowed to sell it or not... Because of the uncertainty, they keep a low profile and don't advertise.'[5] Though this was in 1995, the ambiguity on sales and export of this type of equipment in Europe remains.

Restrictions have begun to be tightened up, both in Europe and the US, with the ban on the export of electro-shock devices that are obviously destined for torturous uses. Yet reporting of the export of all kinds of weapons is very weak. Also, the problems of licensed production and brokering in torture devices are just as pronounced as in small arms. The British Government promised to lead on tightening up the law on brokering in 1998. As this book went to press, a Bill was making very slow progress through legislative channels. For more on electro-shock weapons and their availability, see chapter 7.

Conflict and refugees

Even a cursory glance at where most refugees and internally displaced people come from highlights the obvious connection between war, conflict and people fleeing for a better life – or even to save their life.

Impact on human rights

The United Nations High Commissioner for Refugees (UNHCR) provides protection and assistance to refugees, internally displaced people (IDPs) and asylum seekers. At the start of 2001 the number of people of concern to UNHCR was 21.8 million, one out of every 275 people on earth. That included 12 million refugees, 0.9 million asylum seekers, 0.8 million returned refugees, 6 million internally displaced and 0.4 million returned IDPs, plus 1.7 million others of concern.[6]

Afghans currently constitute the largest single refugee population, at around 3.6 million people. Civilians from the central African state of Burundi constitute the second largest group with 568,000 refugees, and Iraqis are the third at 512,800.[7]

With the changing nature of war in the last few decades, with internal conflicts replacing inter-state wars, the number of IDPs has greatly increased. The

Seeking refuge

Origin and destination of major refugee populations in 1999.

Country of origin	Main countries of asylum	Refugees
Afghanistan	Pakistan / Iran	3,580,400
Burundi	Tanzania	568,000
Iraq	Iran	512,800
Sudan	Uganda / DR Congo / Ethiopia / Kenya / Central African Republic / Chad	490,000
Bosnia-Herzegovina	Yugoslavia / Croatia / US / Sweden / Netherlands / Denmark	478,300
Somalia	Kenya / Ethiopia / Yemen / Djibouti	447,800
Angola	Zambia / DR Congo / Namibia	432,700
Sierra Leone	Guinea / Liberia	400,800
Eritrea	Sudan	376,400
Vietnam	China / US	370,300

Refugees by Numbers 2001 Edition, UNHCR, November 2001.

UN estimates there are some 20-25 million IDPs world-wide, with the most recent large displacement of populations in Eritrea, Colombia, Angola, DRC, Afghanistan, Sri Lanka and Bosnia-Herzegovina – all war-torn countries.

Nationalists and conservatives in the West criticize their governments for accepting refugees from abroad, and call for tighter controls and even detention of asylum seekers. It should be noted that while those states are huge purveyors of arms to the regions from which refugees are fleeing, they are not unduly 'burdened' with the result of their sales. The main host countries for refugees are Pakistan, sheltering 2 million and Iran with 1.9 million. Germany is the main western home to refugees, with 976,000.

Worst human rights abusers:
1 Turkey

Despite its membership of NATO, and its close relationship with the European Union (EU), to which it aspires for membership, Turkey is the worst human-rights abusing state in the European region. There are ongoing tensions between Turkey and Greece, especially over the Turkish occupation of northern Cyprus, but the brutality has been reserved mainly for the ethnic Kurds in the southeast of the country. Since 1984, the Turkish military has been at war against the Kurdish Workers' Party (PKK), a militant Kurdish independent group.

The PKK's tactics have hardly been mild. They include bombings, kidnapping and extortion, but the Turkish response has been the systematic repression of the Kurdish people – some 28 million of whom reside in Turkey. Since the outbreak of the war, more than 37,000 people have been killed, mostly Kurds, and 3 million have been displaced.

Turkey is determined not to allow the Kurdish people to live as Kurds in Turkey. Their political parties are suppressed and their leaders summarily arrested or executed. The ban on speaking their own language has only just been revoked. Journalists expressing sympathy for Kurdish rights have been arrested. More than 3,000 Kurdish villages have been destroyed.

The Turkish military has carried out its repression using weapons supplied by the US and Europe.[8,9] The next biggest supplier is Germany, which has delayed and blocked some arms deals because of Turkey's human rights situation.

For their weapons deals, Turkey demands licensed production and joint production deals in order to boost its own weapons manufacturing industry. The weapons are thus produced in Turkey, away from prying eyes, maintaining jobs there rather than for employees of the licensing company.

Despite current financial crisis, the country is embarking on an 8-year military modernization plan, including the purchase of helicopters, battle tanks, small arms and communication systems. The Turkish Ministry of Defense receives 10 per cent of the national budget, a larger proportion than any other government department.

The latest EU progress report on Turkey, published in November 2001, states that the country has not improved 'the situation as regards torture and mistreatment'. For more on subsidies and licensed production, see chapter 5.

2 Indonesia

Indonesia is the classic example of an anti-democratic, repressive state, sustained in military might by friends in the West hoping to get their hands on rich oil and logging reserves. Since 1965, the country has been led by an autocratic military regime, the father of which was the infamous General Suharto, who ruled for 32 years and oversaw murder, corruption and repression on an unprecedented scale. Following his resignation after the 1997 Asian economic crisis, a string of short ruling presidents replaced him until

Ploughshares Four:
personal disarmament at work

In the early hours of Monday, 29 January 1996, three women snipped their way through the fence of the British Aerospace (BAe) factory in Warton, Lancashire, UK. Soon after, they magically found themselves inside the south hangar, right in front of a Hawk jet destined for Indonesia, where it was to be used against the people of East Timor, who have suffered the loss of more than a third of their population since 1975.

The women took out household hammers and blow by blow disabled all those components and devices that were connected to weaponry – the plane's nose cone, the radar, the bomb attachment under the wings and the control devices in the cockpit. Lotta Kronlid, Andrea Needham and Joanna Wilson then hung up banners, poured seeds and ashes over the wings, put up photographs of children along with a video and a report from their group Seeds of Hope-East Timor Ploughshares. Two hours later, after singing, dancing in front of the security cameras and waving to a patrol that went past they finally phoned the British Press Association from within the hangar asking them to phone security at British Aerospace.

Twenty minutes later they were arrested. Some days later Angie Zelter, the fourth Ploughshare person, was arrested after publicly stating her intention to disarm a Hawk. All four women were on remand at Risley Prison charged with criminal damage and conspiracy to commit damage to the tune of $3.8 million. Their sentences were to be between one and fifteen years. Since their action other Ploughshares women have carried out support and campaigning work. The Ploughshares philosophy is about breaking through fears for personal safety and taking responsibility for actions. All actions are non-violent and 'challenge the sheep-like habit of doing as others do, of not stepping out of line, otherwise known as obedience'.

Six months after the action, a jury stunned the legal profession, arms companies and governments by acquitting the women of causing criminal damage. The court accepted the Ploughshares' defense that they had acted to prevent the crime of genocide. Arguably, the high profile campaign has reduced the quantity of arms that would otherwise have been supplied. ■

From information supplied by Rowan Tilly, Seeds of Hope - East Timor Ploughshares. E-mail: ricarda@gn.apc.org

the current president, Megawati Sukarnoputri took over on 23 July 2001.

While the Indonesian people themselves suffered horribly under the Suharto regime, it was the people of East Timor who were systematically repressed and murdered after Indonesia invaded in December 1975. More than 200,000 people – a third of the population – died during the occupation, which only came to a fragile close following East Timor's referendum for independence in 1999. Even then, Indonesian-backed and armed militia refused to accept the result, and rampaged through the country murdering civilians. The UN estimates 1,500 to 2,000 people were killed, and 75 per cent of the population were forced into hiding. Today, 60,000 to 80,000 people remain in refugee camps in West Timor.

As ever, the West was Indonesia's main arms quartermaster throughout Suharto's reign of terror.

- On 23 March 1997, 7 Timorese youths were killed and 42 wounded when Indonesian security forces in Dili prevented them from meeting with a UN special ambassador.
- During the first 8 months of 1998, there were 37 confirmed extra-judicial killings in East Timor.

Open arms – the West's weaponry relationship with Indonesia

The supply of military equipment to Indonesia (a selection only)

Britain 16 BAe Hawk jets were licensed for Indonesia in 1996, reportedly used for terrorizing East Timor villages.

Indonesia has been described as 'Heckler & Koch' country, because of its use of assault rifles designed by H&K, a British-owned German company.

In December 1996, the Conservative UK Government announced 50 Alvis Scorpion tanks would be supplied, which have guns fitted as standard. The Labour Government has continued the deliveries.

British company GKN has supplied Tactica water cannon.

United States A former major supplier, but imposed an embargo on fighters and similar weapons in 1993, and riot control equipment and small arms in 1994. In 1999, cut off all military ties citing human rights abuses. US weapons manufacturers are keen to resume sales – the top six US weapons companies had contracts worth a total of $60 million when the 1999 embargo was introduced. Military training has continued unabated.

Australia Geographically close to East Timor, but has turned a blind

- During 1998, 18 students were killed on demonstrations that were suppressed using British-supplied Alvis battle tanks.
- In 1991, over 100 people died when Indonesian troops opened fire on demonstrators in the East Timorese capital Dili.
- In early February 1999, 5 people were shot dead by police in the Indonesian province of Aceh as people listened to a speech by the Free Aceh movement.
- In Aceh on 3 May 1999, police opened fire on protesters without warning, continuing to fire as they fled, killing 38.

Many hundreds more examples of Indonesian brutality have been reported.[10]

The use of Western-supplied arms by Indonesia to carry out atrocities both internally, in East Timor and other occupied territories like West Papua, has been prolific.

---

eye to repression there. Since 1978, has approved the Indonesian annexation of the province, and increased military ties ever since. Australian military aid to Indonesia was worth $3.5 million in 1998. After East Timor elections in 1999, condemned Indonesia's actions, and now supplies most troops and support for the peacekeeping mission there.

Aotearoa/New Zealand Refurbished two TA-4J Skyhawks ground attack aircraft (US-built). Severed ties since East Timor referendum.

Russia Stepped in after US embargo on military aircraft, offering fighters and helicopters.

France Rivals Russia for the supply of fighter aircraft. French arms exports to Indonesia in 1998 were worth double the British total of $161.3 million. Was prime mover in lobbying for ending the partial EU arms embargo after East Timor referendum.

Other major suppliers included Germany (submarines), Belgium (fighter upgrades), Sweden (naval cannon), China (riot control equipment). South Africa is also a supplier: in 1998 it provided Indonesia with military support equipment worth $473,000 (R2,597,000). ■

Arms Exports to Indonesia, Campaign Against Arms Trade, October 1999. *South African Export Statistics for Conventional Arms: 1997-1999*, The Directorate of Conventional Arms Control (South Africa).

Short European, British and American arms embargoes were imposed during the aftermath of the East Timorese referendum, but within weeks governments were being lobbied to drop them. Only the US retained the embargo (see below).

3 Saudi Arabia

The Saudi state is illiberal and intolerant, governed by an autocratic and repressive royal family. The practice of any religion except Islam is forbidden and dissent of any kind is heavily punished with the full rigor of *shari'a* (Islamic law). In 1996, Amnesty International noted a sharp increase in executions, at least 192 having been carried out in the preceding year, as well as many floggings and amputations. In 1998, at least 29 people were executed after grossly unfair and secretive trials. Over 80 executions were carried out in the first 8 months of 1999. In late 2001, three men were executed there for being homosexual.

The Saudi regime is a huge arms customer from western nations, and was on the receiving end of the biggest-ever British arms deals. Britain won the Saudis' favor in arms sales following the reluctance of the US Congress to allow large arms deals to the country. The US had been a major supplier, and the UK exploited Congress' reticence. Saudi has extraordinary levels of military spending, funded by rich oil reserves, but also beholden to them.

The multi-billion dollar Al-Yamamah deal, finally signed in February 1986, involved the transfer of tranches of military equipment from Britain, including 72 Tornado fighters, 30 Hawk advanced trainers and 30 Swiss-licensed Pilatus PC-9 trainers, and was paid for with off-set agreements including oil. In July 1988, at the height of a Middle Eastern arms race, Britain signed a second deal, Al-Yamamah II, described as 'the biggest [British] sale of anything to anyone'. It was valued at not less than $24 billion (£16 billion), though much higher sums were predicted in the long term. On the shopping list were up to 50 more Tornadoes, 60 more Hawks and more than 80 helicopters from Westland.

The deal was typically secretive, and both the Conservative and Labour governments have refused to publish an internal report into the deal, which was fraught with allegations of corruption, pay-offs and backhanders. Commentators have said that Britain's reliance on the Saudis as an arms customer through-out the 1980s and 1990s undermined the independence of its government.[11] For more on this, corruption and the Al-Yamamah deals, see chapter 7.

1 *Human Rights Report 2001,* Amnesty International. http://www.web.amnesty.org/web/ar2001. **2** *Dictators or Democracies? US arms transfers to developing countries 1991-1994* & *Arms Un-Control: A record year for US military exports,* Project on Demilitarization and Democracy, August 1995. **3** *The role of the US arms transfers in human rights violations: rhetoric versus reality,* William Hartung, testimony delivered to US subcommittee on International Operations and Human Rights, House International Relations Committee, 7 March 2001. **4** Much of the material in the following section is taken from the excellent Amnesty International report: *Stopping the torture trade,* Amnesty International UK, 2001. The material can also be viewed at www.web.amen-esty.org/web.ttt.nsf/June2001 **5** *Asian Sources Security Products,* November 1995, Vol. 1, issue 3; cited in Stopping the torture trade, Amnesty International UK, 2001. **6** http://www.unhcr.ch/cgi- **7** All figures from *Refugees by Numbers 2001 Edition,* UNHCR, November 2001. www.unhcr.ch **8** *Weapons Transfers and Violations of the Laws of War in Turkey,* Human Rights Watch (New York), November 1995. **9** *US arms sales to Turkey during the Clinton administration,* World Policy Institute & The Federation of American Scientists, October 1999. **10** Reports are easy to come by, but good starting points are: *Arms Exports to Indonesia,* Campaign Against Arms Trade, October 1999 and *Indonesia at the Crossroads,* World Policy Institute, October 2001. **11** *The Arabian Connection, the UK arms trade to Saudi Arabia,* Campaign Against Arms Trade, May 2000.

4 Impact on development

Debt as the legacy of military borrowing... Debt relief and arms sales... How the arms trade affects health, education and other social factors in developing nations... The traffic in weapons, the IMF and globalization.

'IT IS NOT possible for the community of nations to achieve any of its major goals – not peace, not environmental protection, not human rights or democratization, not fertility reduction nor social integration – except in the context of sustainable development that leads to human security.'[1]

The issue of debt and development and the problems created by them, are not new as this statement by the UN Development Program (UNDP) in 1994 shows. Nor are world leaders particularly ignorant of the state of the world in terms of poverty.

In January 2000, the then US president Bill Clinton declared 'the month of Africa' and renewed the country's commitment to finding lasting solutions to the continent's problems of debt and conflict. His successor George W Bush has promised to continue the legacy.

In a rousing speech following the 11 September 2001 attacks, British prime minister Tony Blair promised to make Africa a priority for his second term in government. The continent, he said, was 'a scar on the face of the conscience of the world' and he committed himself to a crusade against poverty there.

As in most arms sales issues, however, rhetoric rarely matches reality. Arms sales, conflict and world poverty are so intimately connected as to be almost indistinct. Those same world leaders who shed a tear for the poor and starving in Africa also help sustain the conflict and poverty which infect the continent.

The new European Code of Conduct on Arms Sales

(see chapter 8), which was finally introduced in 1998 after many years of lobbying by campaigners, urges arms-selling European states to consider 'whether the proposed export would seriously hamper the sustainable development of the recipient country' when granting arms export licenses. But the Code has had little effect, so far, in preventing arms exports to some of the poorest and most underdeveloped nations.

Despite improvements over the past few decades, there are still an estimated 1.3 billion people who live in deepest poverty. According to the World Bank, the minimum requirement for a basic standard of living is an annual income of $370. In 1997, the average per capita income across Africa was $350 a year, and of course that does not mean that each person actually receives such a sum: the World Bank's figure is an average.

The poorest countries in the world are so poor largely because of huge debts owed to the developed world, much as repayments for past arms sales. Many of the most heavily indebted countries are currently engaged in, or emerging from, conflict of some kind.

Arms sales fuel a never-ending vicious cycle of poverty and debt. During the Cold War, developing nations found themselves filing in behind one or the other of the major world powers, buying or receiving free arms to strengthen their position. This in turn fuelled local arms races.

At the same time, dictators and corrupt governments were making large-scale arms purchases, both to bolster their own power and to line their pockets with generous kickbacks and bribes from each sale. High military spending reduced outlay on development and increased the occurrence of cross-border and internal conflicts. This created a need for more arms, which were bought using Western loans, thereby adding to the country's debt.

Post Cold War, the cycle continues in many parts of Africa and Asia. In some regions, nations are suffering the economic effects of decades of borrowing, crushed under the weight of debts that do not really belong to them, which they have no hope of ever paying off.

Debt, the Cold War legacy

At the height of the Cold War in the 1970s and 1980s, the world's poorest regions were caught up in an arms race that is, arguably, the foundation for their poverty today. Central America, the Horn of Africa, southern Africa and Indo-China were drawn into the tensions, which exacerbated regional arms races and localized conflicts. In 1985, Nicaragua allocated 26.2 per cent of government spending to the military, Mozambique spent 38 per cent, El Salvador 29.1 per cent, Ethiopia 28.9 per cent and Iran 34.1 per cent. In most cases, arms purchases meant military expenditure had to be increased and budgets for development were tightened. In other cases, the countries borrowed hard currency from international lenders to fund their arms purchases, or simply went into debt with the arms supplying nation.

According to a report by the Campaign Against Arms Trade (CAAT), 'With the end of the Cold War, the Southern African region has witnessed the withdrawal of superpower intervention, the end of apartheid, the termination of conflict in Namibia and Mozambique, a 30 per cent decline in regional military expenditure and the demobilization of tens of thousands of soldiers. However, the debts and costs of destruction that accumulated during the Cold War will remain a burden for generations to come. Children not yet born will have to pay the price of debt for wars they did not fight, for ideas they do not hold, for a regional and global system that no longer exists and for decisions made by regional and world leaders no longer in power.'[2]

According to a Jubilee 2000 report, one-fifth of all developing country debt consists of loans given to dictators.[3] The report says the lenders, not the countries currently crushed by former regimes' debts, should be

Cold War, hot sales, low growth

Cold War expenditure on arms had a dramatic effect on sub-Saharan African nations. Across the region, the average annual percentage growth rate fell as a result of the Cold War-fuelled arms races and regional conflicts.

Country	Average annual percentage economic growth rate 1975-84	1985-89	1990-97
Angola	—	4.7	−1.6
Burundi	3.8	5.1	−2.8
Cameroon	8.5	−0.1	−0.9
Congo, Democratic Republic	−0.3	1.7	−6.7
Ethiopia	—	4.1	3.5
Gambia	4.3	3.3	2.4
Kenya	4.7	5.9	2.1
Mozambique	—	6.0	4.2
Rwanda	6.8	2.9	−5.5
Sierra Leone	2.0	0.8	−3.3
Zambia	0.2	2.3	−0.4

The arms trade, debt and development, Susan Willett, Campaign Against Arms Trade, May 1999.

held responsible. CAAT's excellent report on the arms trade and development, cited earlier, reveals that countries which are poverty stricken because of the military spending of their former dictators include Bolivia, Central African Republic, Chad, DRC (Zaire), Kenya, Liberia, Mali, Myanmar (Burma), Uganda and Zambia.

Current military spending and arms sales

Despite their being locked into this poverty trap, poorer nations are still regarded as legitimate and profitable arms customers for Western states which helped create their situation.

According to a report for the US congress, arms sales to developing countries together far outweigh arms sales to developed countries.[4] According to their definition, countries of the South accounted for 66 per cent of the value of all international arms deliveries in 2000.

Figures are hard to come by. In 1996, no African state reported its military expenditure to the UN. But according to the International Institute for Strategic Studies (IISS), in 1997 sub-Saharan African expenditure on the military was $8.8 billion, around 3.3 per cent of the regional GDP. Sudan's spending on the military accounts for some 80 per cent of government expenditure. Military spending in Central and South Asia was $19.2 billion in 1997, with India and Pakistan jointly accounting for around 80 per cent of that.

Debt relief and arms sales

A progressive attitude towards helping developing countries emerge from the cycle of debt and conflict depends on a two handed approach. Firstly, Western nations must write off the huge, unpayable debts owed to them by the very poorest nations. Secondly, they should cease selling arms to those countries, thereby preventing new debts from accumulating and helping at least to stem the flow of weapons which fuels the war and conflicts which exacerbate poverty.

The UN Development Program (UNDP) maintains that 'countries spending very little on defense and

---

Export credits: the direct connection between arms sales and debt

All established arms selling countries run insurance schemes for their arms companies to make sure corporations get their money, even if the purchasing country defaults on payments. In many cases, it is these 'export credits' which directly create debt for arms buying countries in the developing world.

When the developing nation cannot afford to pay for a shipment of arms they have received, the selling government pays its arms companies and the debt is transferred to the government.

A large percentage of British bilateral debts have been incurred in this way, through their Export Credits Guarantee Department (ECGD). Between 1994 and 1997, 20 per cent of all British export credits were extended to arms sales. More recently the figure has been much higher at around half, while defense equipment made up only 2 per cent of exports. For more on export credits, see chapter 5. ■

---

much more on human development have been much more successful at defending their national sovereignty than those spending heavily on arms.'[5]

Britain has led worldwide on the cancellation of developing world debt – providing high levels of aid to Uganda ($117 million in 2000) and Mozambique ($63.5 million), with barely any arms sales. But too often, the values of the country's Department for International Development (DfID) are overruled, or negated, by the gung-ho arms sales policy of the Prime Minister. Through DfID, Britain gave South Africa $43 million to help eradicate poverty and inequality in 2000. In the same year, Britain granted export licenses to sell weapons to South Africa worth $91.5 million, more than double the amount for aid.

Social impacts of conflict

The servicing of debt for arms sales obviously affects health and education, and has other social impacts in

---

Africa's big spenders

Selected military spending in 1997 and 1998.

Country	Year	Military spending	As percentage of government spending
Botswana	1998	$323 million/£222 million	11.5 %
Namibia	1998	$89 million/£61 million	—
Angola	1998	$380 million/£262 million	10 %
Mozambique	1998	—	19.4 %
Zimbabwe	1997/98	$456 million/314 million	—
South Africa	Each of the years 1996-1999	$1.9 billion/£1.3 billion	—
Uganda	1998	$153 million/£105 million	—
Tanzania	1998	$311 million/£214 million	23 %

The US, Europe, China and Russia account for the vast bulk of arms sales to all of these developing regions. Israel, Brazil and South Africa are also large suppliers.

Between 1989 and 1996, the value of all arms transfer agreements with developing nations comprised 67.5 per cent of the world total. In 1996, the transfers were worth $19.4 billion.

The arms trade, debt and development, Susan Willett, Campaign Against Arms Trade, May 1999.

Arms deals

Arms deliveries to the world, 1993-2000: leading suppliers compared (in US$ millions).

Rank	Supplier	Deliveries value 1993-1996
1	United States	124,206
2	United Kingdom	42,400
3	France	26,900
4	Russia	23,100
5	Germany	12,600
6	Sweden	7,000
7	China	5,500
8	Israel	4,000
9	Ukraine	2,500
10	Italy	2,400
11	Canada	2,300

US Government

the developing world. Money spent on arms, or money spent servicing debts, means less money is spent in social and developmental programs within the country.

At a more local level, conflict and the proliferation of small arms in developing nations have a pronounced impact on health, education and other social services, as research by development charity Oxfam has illustrated.[6]

The charity carried out research in Uganda and the DRC, looking at the impact of conflict and small arms on the human situation there.

In the Kitgum district of Uganda, for example, the insecurity caused by small arms has had a profound adverse effect on the delivery of the health service there.

The armed rebel group, the Lord's Resistance Army (LRA), armed with light weapons sourced from Sudan, has targeted hospitals and health centers to obtain drugs, and has even kidnapped medical staff to treat its own soldiers. Conflict has also disrupted monitoring of health problems and vaccination pro-

The $6 billion South Africa arms deal

South Africa is by no means the poorest nation in Africa, but it is a country with severe financial and social problems that is still a major arms customer. In 1997, it had a per capita income of $3,400 but with great discrepancies between rich and poor. Nearly 20 per cent of the adult population was illiterate, and roughly 50 per cent was unemployed. The post-apartheid economic split between white and black in the country is still obvious and the scale of crime in the country is so high that it deters foreign investors.

Despite chronic poverty, the ANC-led Government, under Thabo Mbeki, announced in 1999 that it would embark on a major rearmament of the South African National Defense Force.

The program includes the purchase, over 15 years, of 52 fighter planes from a BAE Systems and SAAB consortium, 7 patrol boats and submarines from German-led consortia, 4 super-Lynx helicopters from British led GKN-Westland, and 40 light helicopters from the Italian firm Agusta.

When it was first arranged, the rearmament was valued at between $5-6 billion (£3-£4 billion). The cost is twice the country's housing budget and ten times the amount set aside to deal with HIV/AIDS, two of its most severe development problems. Before the contracts were finalized, South Africa's treasury warned the Government that the purchases would be risky and would use up much of recent public spending increases.

But the price of the weapons has effectively almost doubled because of the collapse of the rand. At the start of January 2002 the currency was down to 40 per cent of what it had been worth against the dollar when the deal was struck. The contract is to be paid for in dollars, euros and pounds. Even the large-scale off-sets of inward investment in South Africa, which the ANC promised would result in 65,000 jobs, are now unlikely to emerge because of the currency collapse and the problems of crime and enforcing the agreement.*

South Africa has reduced the original order, and is reportedly attempting to back out of buying so many aircraft. Yet Western arms companies pursued the deal with gusto. The Germans and French lavished attention on influential ANC MPs, the British BAE Systems donated around $700,000 to an ANC war veterans' association, and paid for South African trade unionists to take holiday trips in England and Sweden to ensure their support.

There are also accusations of widespread corruption in the deal, involving arms company executives and government officials. Questions have also been asked about why South Africa needs military submarines. Mr Mbeki has told reporters the country needs to protect its waters from trawlers that loot fish off its coast. (See also box p 115.) ∎

*'Politics and Principles', Chris McGreal, *The Guardian (UK)*, 7 January 2002.

grams in the region, resulting in child deaths from curable and preventable diseases like diarrhea, cholera and respiratory infections. Hospitals are overstretched, at times, with casualties from the insurgence.

Small arms and localized conflict have also affected health provision in the Ituri district of the DR Congo (DRC). Hospitals are starved to breaking point as a result of government spending on the war. Eight out of 18 districts in Ituri have no doctor. Most districts have no vehicles, no refrigerators and no electricity. The only time that nurses and doctors received state salaries in the last ten years was in July 1998.

Bubonic plague, which used to infect 20 to 30 people in the region annually before the 1996 renewal of fighting, infected 53 people in 1999 and 207 from June to October 2000, including 48 deaths.

Education in the developing world is also badly affected. In the rural parts of Kitgum, Uganda, education has been interrupted also as a result of insecurity caused by widespread small arms use. Insurgency has displaced rural people, who have to be educated in overcrowded, under-resourced, displaced schools in permanent displacement camps. School attendance is irregular because of frequent inter-ethnic cattle raids. Teachers, who can't enforce discipline because their pupils have guns, often face robbery of their wages and school funds.

The conflict in neighboring DRC means the Government no longer has contact with schools in the east, where the rebel authorities have not instituted education programs following their insurgency. Civil servants in the DRC Ministry of Education explain that the lack of funding now given to education across the country is because of priority being given to the war effort. Primary teachers in the North Kivu region have not been paid state salaries since 1995.

Three out of ten Congolese children never attended school in the year 1999 to 2000, the rest attended only sporadically. Boys seemed keener to join groups of armed bandits who steal, take drugs and support rebel groups, than go to school. Girls are often forced to sell their bodies to get enough money to pay their school fees.

In DRC's Djugu territory, the war of 1999 to 2000 had a devastating impact on schools. 211 schools out of 228 were burnt or closed because of the fighting. Many of the children they taught were forced to flee, or were killed in the conflict. And war has other deleterious human consequences in the world's poorest states.

For example, children in the developing world are the most profoundly affected by the proliferation of small arms and combat. They suffer trauma from witnessing so much bloodshed and human rights abuse, and become orphans when their families are caught up in war. Orphaned children become more vulnerable to poverty, and are often forced into child labor or prostitution.

Women are also badly affected. Conflict exposes them to all sorts of violence, including rape and sexually transmitted diseases. As seen earlier, small arms in the Kitgum region of Uganda have rendered the delivery of social services dangerous and difficult, so children, women and old people are prevented from receiving the assistance they need.

Conflict also affects food and water supplies. Cattle are slaughtered or stolen, water contaminated and crops burned as part of internal conflicts. People become reliant on food relief from international agencies. But food relief conduits are themselves subject to looting, security difficulties and the political machinations of the warring factions.

The arms trade, globalization and free trade

The growth of the global justice/anti-globalization movement over recent years has begun to illustrate the interconnectedness of some of the world's most urgent problems including human and resource exploitation, climate change, war and conflict, human rights abuse and the north-south economic divide.

The arms trade cannot be fully understood in isolation from all these problems, though it is often much simpler to regard it as a problem in its own right (see chapter 8). Like most industries, arms companies have reaped the benefits of globalization in a number of ways.

Firstly, improvements in technology have meant that arms firms have become truly global – international travel, communication and finance have become so simple now as to be almost irrelevant. Like companies manufacturing sports equipment and toys, arms manufacturers have become 'plug-in industries' locating their production lines to open up new arms markets, and wherever labor and tax is cheapest, environmental requirements are non-existent, employment regulations are weakest and regulations for the export of armaments are most easily obtained.

Arms corporations have become unregulated transnational monoliths, rather than state-controlled and supervised companies.

The New York based World Policy Institute and Stephen Staples, a founder member of the International Network on Disarmament and Globalization, have shown that the global move towards deregulation and free trade has been a gift for the arms industry.[7] It is able to reap the benefits of international agreements to break down trade barriers, drawn up at the World Trade Organization (WTO) and similar bodies, while being subject to few of the restrictions they impose and the standards they demand.

Global agreements to liberalize trade are drawn up, in the main, to benefit Western companies, who are able to complain if they believe they are subject to unfair barriers to trade. The WTO forced the European Union (EU) to open its markets to hor-

HIPCs and SAPs

As described above, some countries are so poor and in so much debt that they can never hope to even pay the interest on their debts, let alone meet the debt itself. In 1996, the World Bank and IMF launched the Heavily Indebted Poor Countries (HIPC) initiative, which was intended to help countries trapped in this position. It aimed to both reduce their debt burden, and give some relief to countries to improve their ability to generate income.

But from the very start, the initiative was set up in order to keep dept payments flowing to Western nations. It contained very few moves towards encouraging the writing-off of those debts altogether.

The HIPC initiative aimed to bring a country's debt burden to sustainable levels in terms of what the country could earn in goods exports. But in order to qualify for debt relief, the countries have to impose certain internal policies, including structural adjustment programs (SAPs), tightening budgets on health and education spending. The IMF also insists on caps on military spending.

Critics argue the qualifying terms and conditions that HIPCs have to meet are too stringent, and prioritize monetary value above human development goals. The priority of the initiative is to ensure payment to some creditors, rather than concentrating on the financial recovery of the nation. Even savings made from reducing military spending have to be redirected towards debt serving, rather than on development.

According to debt campaign organization JubileePlus, after five years, 'only three countries have come through all the HIPC stages (implemented IMF programs and so on) and been given the 'enhanced' debt relief promised at Cologne in 1999'. Those countries are Uganda, Bolivia and Mozambique.

Oxfam has called for the introduction of a cap on debt repayments of no more than 10 per cent of government revenues, arguing that creditors should offer incentives for countries willing to transfer savings from debt relief into schools, clinics and water supplies. ∎

www.jubileeplus.org/databank/Briefings/HIPC3001001.htm
The arms trade, debt and development, Susan Willett, Campaign Against Arms Trade, May 1999.

mone-treated beef after the US challenged the EU's ban on the product. However, the WTO also ruled that the US Clean Air Act, which requires oil refineries to produce cleaner petroleum/gas to protect the environment, was an unfair barrier to Venezuela's petroleum/gas trade.

Countries are prevented by international trade rules

from unfairly supporting their own industries above the industries of other nations. Caribbean countries are not allowed to give financial aid to their banana industry on which the region depends, because it is unfair competition for the American-owned banana

---

Tanzania's $40 million air traffic control system

In December 2001, the issue of British arms sales to Tanzania erupted in the British press. The case is a good example of the pursuing of arms deals, even though the sales are plainly bad for the poverty-stricken recipient country.

The country has a per capita income of just $245 a year. Half the population lacks access to clean water, and one in four children die before their fourth birthday.

In 2000, Britain contributed $92 million in aid to the country, part of international aid totaling $245 million. The World Bank and International Monetary Fund (IMF) have developed a debt relief package worth $2.9 billion for the country. Britain has written off $144 million of the debt that Tanzania owed it.

Despite Tanzania's poverty, the British Government approved the license for the export to Tanzania of a military air traffic control system, manufactured by BAE Systems, costing $40 million. The deal is to be financed by a loan from British Barclays Bank.

Even the World Bank and IMF criticized the deal. A report commissioned by the World Bank from the International Civil Aviation Authority, leaked to the British press in July 2002, said Tanzania could buy a civilian system for an eighth of the cost. The British system would not even cover all of the east African country's civil aviation needs, according to the report, which concluded the system was old, inappropriate and unworkable.

Despite protest from both the Department for International Development (DfID) and even British Chancellor Gordon Brown, the Prime Minister Tony Blair insisted the delivery would go ahead, arguing that it would safeguard 250 British jobs. But it later emerged that the equipment had already been built, under assurances from ministers that the export license would be a mere administrative matter.

A government adviser told the British *Guardian* newspaper, 'the Prime Minister has proudly talked about his Africa initiative. If he really cares about Africa this is a test case for him.'[8] Tony Blair's bullish attitude towards the Tanzania deal is in direct contrast to his promise to be a new friend to Africa. ■

'Just what they need – a £28m air defence system', David Hencke and Larry Elliott, *The Guardian (UK)*, 18 December 2001.

industry in Central and South America. The Global Agreement on Trade and Services (GATS), which is currently being pushed through the WTO, intends to extend these kinds of rules to other areas such as water, healthcare and education provision.

But at the WTO, and in all other global agreements, the military is specifically excluded from the rules governing global trade. The main WTO governing document, the General Agreement on Tariffs and Trade (GATT), states that a country cannot be prevented from taking any action 'it considers necessary for the protection of its essential security interests... relating to the traffic in arms, ammunition and implements of war and such traffic in other goods and materials as is carried on directly for the purpose of supplying a military establishment.'

In other words, the WTO GATT and other trade agreements do not apply to the arms trade. There are no international restrictions on what munitions a country can buy or sell, how much these should cost, how much a country can spend, who they buy weapons from or to what extent they subsidize their own arms industry. This process has contributed to the pattern of rich countries becoming richer, and poorer nations staying poor, or becoming poorer.

Western nations are not prevented by WTO rules from subsidizing their own arms industries, and so are able to acquire military equipment at artificially low knock-down prices, while keeping the finance within the country. Moreover, the exclusion from WTO regulations means they can buy arms domestically, even when other countries are offering better products more cheaply.

Developing nations rarely have established arms industries and so buy their weaponry from abroad at a cost often way above what the equipment is worth, draining yet more money out of the country. Even when there is a local arms industry, this is usually so small that buying abroad remains cheaper. Developing nations pump cash into their own arms industries too, in attempts to improve their economies, because it is the only industry they can legally support in this way.

When seeing how trade rules benefit the rich countries, especially in the arms arena, it is not surprising that airplane and arms manufacturer Boeing was the prime sponsor of the WTO meeting in Seattle in 1999.

Global agreements to break down barriers to trade are having the effect of preventing developing and middle income countries from exploiting the resources they do have to trade on the world market, keeping those countries financially subordinate to the rich West. For more on globalization, see *The No-Nonsense Guide to Globalization*.

1 *UNDP Human Development Report,* Oxford University Press, 1994. **2** *The arms trade, debt and development,* Susan Willett, Campaign Against Arms Trade, May 1999. **3** *Dictators and debt,* J Hanlon, Jubilee 2000 Report, November 1998, cited in *The arms trade, debt and development.* **4** Conventional Arms Transfers to Developing Nations, 1993-2000, Richard F. Grimmett, Congressional Research Service Report for Congress, 16 August 2001. **5** *UNDP Human Development Report,* Oxford University Press, 1994. **6** *Conflict's children: the human cost of small arms in Kitgum and Kotido, Uganda* & *Under Fire: the human cost of small arms in northeast Democratic Republic of Congo,* Oxfam, January 2001. **7** *The WTO and the globalization of the arms industry,* World Policy Institute, New York, December 1999.

5 Who really pays for the arms trade?

Direct and indirect government subsidies... Jobs in the industry and the problems of joint production... How tax payers subsidize the arms business.

LIKE MANY COUNTRIES, Britain has a law banning foreigners convicted of a serious crime from visiting the country. In 1998, American boxer Mike Tyson, a convicted rapist, wanted to fight a British challenger. A short spat ensued between liberals led by women's groups, who argued Tyson shouldn't be allowed into Britain, and politicians who didn't want to offend the American people. Unsurprisingly, the politicians won out. They argued that staging the boxing match would create jobs and generate income. Tyson's promoter told a British radio journalist: it's not as if he's an arms dealer, we let arms dealers in every day!

The argument that the arms trade creates or sustains jobs, or brings money into the national economy, is one of the most difficult arguments campaigners face. These arguments have strong political currency – people don't vote for governments that threaten their livelihood – but they are based on a fallacy which is only now becoming fully apparent.

The arms trade is an immoral business that causes death, maiming, human rights abuses and suffering around the world. It is also a business that does not bring huge economic or employment benefits to the biggest arms-exporting countries. In many cases, high government subsidies, tax breaks, insurance schemes and promotion for arms manufacturers cost governments more money than weapons producers generate for them.

Countries are artificially propping up their arms industries while refusing to explore fully the potential for diversification into areas that are not only more productive and socially positive but also economically viable. (For more on this see chapter 8).

The extent of government subsidies

Governments subsidize their arms sector in a number of ways. The difficult job for campaigners and academics is to show by how much, and why it is a bad thing.

Information, such as how much a government spends on its own armed forces, what procurement decisions it makes, how much it spends on military research and development and how much export credit insurance it provides for arms companies, is usually secret or difficult to obtain.

Strong, well-informed estimates based on obtainable information are usually the best that campaigners can muster before issuing the challenge to governments: if we are wrong, it falls to you to prove how wrong. After all, if arms exports *are* big earners for state economies, wouldn't politicians be shouting it from the roof tops?

With that proviso in mind, valiant attempts to look at this issue have been made.

In the US, the defense and foreign aid budgets are the largest single source of federal funding to private corporations. According to the World Policy Institute, more than half of all US weapons sales are financed by taxpayers instead of by foreign arms purchasers.[1] During the fiscal year of 1996 (the last year for which figures were available) the US Government spent more than $7.9 billion to help companies secure just over $12 billion in agreements for new international arms sales. In the US, even the Presidential Advisory Board on Arms Proliferation has said government subsidies for arms exports should be phased out.

The report of a Commission of Enquiry (*Mission d'information*) into the control of arms exports in France found that selling weapons overseas does not necessarily result in a net gain for the French economy.

A fact-finding panel established by the French parliament found that no government organization had been able to prove conclusively that France's hefty arms exports were financially beneficial. 'It is by no means certain these sales earn money,' it stated, adding 'France may be offering goods below costs' in order to protect jobs in the country's defense industry. The panel called on France to set up a watchdog agency to assess the economic impact of arms sales each year.

In Britain, *The Subsidy Trap*[2] study by researchers at the Oxford Research Group and the Saferworld organization calculated 'identifiable subsidies to British arms exports to be around £420 million [$605 million] per annum.' This did not include indirect subsidies of companies' research and development amounting to up to £570 million ($821 million) a year.

'We estimate that there is an annual government subsidy specifically to arms exports of over £4,600 [$6,600] for every export-related job maintained,'

Lending a helping hand

A breakdown of how Britain subsidizes its defense export business, in £m.

Net subsidy	£m*
Net cost of supporting military export credits by accepting risk	327
DESO[a] net operating cost via Export Credit Guarantee Dept.	23
Use of MoD[b] personnel to promote sales	14
Support by embassy staff and offices	10
Defense attachés	23
Official visits	29
Tax breaks on bribes and other corrupt practices	92
Direct distortion of procurement choices	86
TOTAL net subsidy for military exports	**604**

*£1= approx. $1.44

[a]DESO = Defence Export Services Organization   [b]MoD = Ministry of Defence

The Subsidy Trap: British Government Financial Support for Arms Exports and the Defence Industry, Ingram and Davies, ORG & Saferworld, July 2001.

Corporate Welfare for Weapons Makers: The Hidden Costs of Spending on Defense and Foreign Aid, William D. Hartung, Policy Analysis August 1999.

Hidden hand

A breakdown of how the US subsidizes its defense export business, in millions of US$.

Agency	Expenditure $m
Financing Aid Programs	
US Department of Defense	
Foreign military financing (FMF)	3,317.8
Defense Export Loan Guarantee fund	16.7
Forgiven / bad loans	1,000.0
Excess defense articles / emergency drawdowns	750.0
No-cost leases of US equipment	63.2
Repeal or waiver of recruitment fees	200.0
US Agency for International Development:	
Economic Support Funds	2,042.3
Export-Import Bank Loans	33.7
Subtotal	**7,423.7**
Promotional and Support Programs	
US Departments of Defense, State, and Commerce	
Government personnel costs for promotion / support	410.0
Government support for air shows / weapons	34.2
Subtotal	444.2
Total: All US government support for arms sales	**7,867.9**

noted Paul Ingram and Dr Ian Davis in the report. British economist and journalist Samuel Brittan has argued convincingly of an 'inflated view of the role of arms and export promotion in the British economy'.[3]

Direct subsidies

Governments' direct financial support for their arms exports can be roughly placed into a few distinct categories. Each of these subsidies results in taxpayers' money being spent, or risked, helping foreign governments to buy arms.

Export promotion – The major arms-exporting countries each year spend huge amounts of money all over the world promoting and marketing their domestic arms companies' products. Export promotion ranges from diplomatic visits by politicians to the provision of advice and support for companies marketing their systems, to regular attendance and promotion at arms exhibitions and conferences.

At the US Pentagon, nearly 6,000 people were employed in 1996 to promote, broker, administer and finance arms sales abroad, at a cost of $378.2 million. In the State Department a further 75 personnel were employed, part of a defense export promotion budget of $3.7 million. And the US commerce department also plays a role, publishing 'defense market assessments' such as *How to do business in Indonesia,* and mounting US presence at foreign arms exhibitions. During 1996, the US Government sent equipment and personnel to 19 overseas weapons shows, at a cost of more than $5.1 million.

Britain has a specific government organization for promoting arms exports, the Defence Export Services Organization (DESO). Its role is 'maximizing legitimate British defense exports in co-ordination with industry'. In 1998/99, DESO had a net operating cost of over $23 million. British Ministry of Defence (MoD) staff are also used to promote military exports, to demonstrate equipment and to provide support for arms exporting companies. Ingram and Davis estimate the use of MoD staff in this way costs $14.4 million a year. Their report also estimates that the cost of the role of defense attachés and foreign office attachés in promoting defense exports amounts to $23 million a year.

Export credits – Government insurance schemes to compensate arms companies when their foreign clients default on payment generally make up the bulk of the government direct subsidies. They also provide financing support for deals. Governments then attempt to recoup the cost from the defaulting nations, with usually only limited success. Often the companies insist on some kind of insurance or guarantee from their home government before embarking on large weaponry export deals. Arms sales make up large proportions of the export credits extended in many major arms exporting countries.

The Export Credits Guarantee Department (ECGD), according to Ingram and Davis, provides a net subsidy of $327 million a year from the British Government for the UK arms industry. Export credit guarantees (ECG) for arms exports outweigh cover for all other British exports. While the arms trade accounts for only 2 per cent of British exports, it has absorbed nearly 30 per cent of ECG cover over the last five years. In 2001, it was around 50 per cent.

Between 1995 and 1998, roughly one-fifth of all export credit cover provided by the French agency, COFACE, went to arms exports, amounting to 11,650 million euros (approx. $10,600 million) in total.

German export credits, through their agency Hermes, have been granted for arms shipments to Indonesia, Turkey, Algeria, Kuwait, the Philippines and South Korea, illustrating the problem of governments financially supporting arms exports to countries with human rights and development problems (see chapters 1 and 4).

The US Export-Import Credit Bank, which could be seen as the equivalent of an export credit organization, is usually prohibited from guaranteeing arms deals (though not always – Congress occasionally makes exceptions). However the US more than makes up for it in other loans and funding programs which subsidize US arms exporters.

The US Foreign Military Financing Program (FMF) received $3.35 billion in 1999 to support grants and loans for the provision of US military equipment and services to more than 24 countries. Recipients of FMF grants in recent years have included Egypt, Israel, Jordan, Turkey and the Ukraine. More funds were allocated for Africa. Another $16 million of subsidy is granted through the US Defense Export Loan Guarantee fund.

Export credits are of particular concern to arms trade campaigners because as well as subsidizing arms companies, they are a large contributor to the debt problems of the developing world (see chapter 4).

In 2001, a sub-body of the Organization for Economic Co-operation and Development (OECD) – a 'rich man's club' of Western nations – responded to a request by G8 leaders* to issue guidance on the granting of export credits for projects in the world's poorest countries.

The OECD Export Credit Group agreed to a statement of principles, designed to discourage the provision of officially supported credits for 'unproductive' expenditure in Heavily Indebted Poor Countries (HIPCs). The statement read: 'The measure seeks to ensure that non-essential capital goods and projects which do not contribute to the social and/or economic development of the poorest nations, but have the effect of increasing their external debt burdens, do not benefit from OECD governments' support.'[4]

While this new approach was welcomed by activists, they did express reservations that it contained no calls for governments to be more transparent in their granting of export credits, and that it only applies to narrowly defined participants in the HIPC initiative.

Nevertheless, the move does show that governments are beginning to listen to campaigners' concerns that export credits may not be financially productive either for granting governments or for recipient countries. Indeed, led by the UK, some arms selling countries are now improving their reporting procedures and transparency (see chapter 8).

Spending distortions – governments also artificially support their arms industries by distorting their own spending on domestic military purchases. They buy

*G8 are the world's wealthiest countries: US, UK, Canada, France, Germany, Italy and Japan, plus Russia.

more arms from domestic suppliers than really needed, they pay more than these ought to cost, and they
choose domestic arms suppliers even if foreign-made
equipment is cheaper and better. In any other industry, World Trade Organization rules and other
free-trade legislation would prevent such spending distortions as unfair competition. But as we have seen
earlier, the military is exempt from international
agreements on trade.

Ingram and Davis estimate that the value of this
process in UK support for defense exports is around
$86.4 million a year. Politicians and civil servants freely
admit their preference for 'buying British' to maintain
the British defense industry.

In a report by the World Policy Institute, William
Hartung decries this kind of spending in the US, which
he calls 'defense pork'. He argues that politicians add
unnecessary and expensive military equipment purchases to the Pentagon's budget in order to please
arms companies, secure or create jobs and so gain
campaign donations and votes. In 1998, $3.8 billion
was added by senators and officials to the amount that
the Pentagon had said it needed to meet its own
defense plans. While most 'defense pork' is US-bought
– so not an arms *export* subsidy – the example shows
how political pressure distorts procurement decisions.

Other subsidies

The above are just three *direct* financial subsidies
which governments provide for their arms industries.
But there are many different ways that governments
indirectly financially support their arms industries, and
while it is more difficult to quantify this kind of support in concrete terms, the benefits to arms companies
can be quite considerable.

Research and development (R&D) – Governments
spend large portions of their defense budgets on
research and development of new weapons systems,

which they contract arms companies to carry out on their behalf.

In 1998/99, the three big US weapons manufacturers received over $8 billion in R&D funding. Ingram and Davis estimate that the arms-export-related portion of British R&D funding for arms manufacturers amounts to a subsidy of up to $821 million a year for the UK arms industry.

Governments justify this expenditure by arguing that it will produce better weapons systems for domestic armed forces, and the costs will be recouped by levying an appropriate charge on exports of the new weapons systems.

The argument is suspect for a number of reasons. Extra charges cannot just be added onto the cost of equipment for export, because the arms export business is such a competitive one – the market forces weapons systems to be exported at near marginal cost.

Also, weapons systems developed with government money are designed and built specifically to meet that government's needs, and often require major modifications (and therefore more cost) before export.

Commissions and bribes – According to one World Bank estimate, the sums distributed worldwide each year as pay-offs and bribes total $80 billion. Campaign group Transparency International (TI) has surveyed attitudes to corruption in business, and found that arms and construction companies were perceived to be the most likely to pay bribes.[5]

Other methods of indirect subsidy include when governments give away still useful 'surplus' arms to foreign governments as sweeteners to buy other products; and government grants and subsidies to help arms producers merge or enter into joint partnerships.

Joint production and off-sets

Quite apart from the amount of subsidies that governments provide, directly or indirectly, to their arms industries, there are other characteristics of the arms trade which belie the argument that selling arms is good for national economies and employment.

The first is that increasingly arms purchasing countries insist on joint and licensed production of weapons systems. Foreign governments too want to create jobs in their local economies, so they arrange for part or even all of the systems to be built locally. Arms companies are often happy to oblige, since most sales go to developing or middle income countries where labor can be cheaper and employment standards lower than the corporation would face at home. While some domestic jobs are certainly created or sustained by large weapons contracts, the export of weapons increasingly involves the export of jobs.

The relationship between the US and Turkey is a good example of this in action. Around $10.5 billion in US weaponry has been delivered to Turkey since the outbreak of the war with the Kurdish PKK group there (see chapter 3) in 1984. Some 77 per cent – $8 billion – of the financing for those weapons purchases has come in grants and loans from the US Government. And the largest deals – of 240 F-16 fighters and 1,698 armored vehicles – involve co-production in Turkey as a condition of the sale. Turkey has an F-16 assembly plant in Ankara employing 2,000 workers.

Buying planes with frozen chickens

Another of the arms trade's modern characteristics blows the myth that it brings large amounts of money into national economies. Many purchasing countries today demand that the vendor bring investment and business into their country as part of the deal. 'Off-set agreements' often mean that the selling country agrees to buy a certain amount of goods from the purchasing country, or promises to invest certain amounts in industries, both military and non military, in the recipient country. An example is the US McDonnell Douglas corporation that once agreed to accept frozen chickens as part-payment (off-set) from Thailand for eight F-15 fighter aircraft.

Current estimates reveal that the value of off-sets needed to secure US arms exports amounts to half the value of the military exports themselves. The recent arms deal between European countries and South Africa has huge off-set arrangements. Britain and Sweden have, for example, promised off-set deals with South Africa for up to four times the value of the 28 Gripen aircraft they are supplying.

Off-sets take money out of the arms-selling country's economy because they involve investment in the purchasing country. They also generate employment in the purchasing country, because workers are needed to produce and supply the goods the vendor has promised to buy as part of the deal. Far from creating jobs in the selling country, off-set deals necessarily create them elsewhere.

American workers lose jobs under off-set arrangements, according to a study for the Presidential Commission on Off-sets in International Trade. A survey of 64 transactions by the eight largest US aerospace companies over the period 1993-98, revealed that direct off-sets supplanted $2.3 billion of US work, the equivalent of 4,200 full-time jobs per year.[6]

Jobs in the arms industry

Off-set deals and joint procurement aside, a further argument – that the weapons business is a thriving employer – is also false.

In chapter 1 it was seen that the global arms industry has been gradually shrinking since the end of the Cold War. Linked to this, the number of people employed in the sector has also fallen.

Moreover, the argument that a government should spend huge amounts of money propping up an industry to safeguard a relatively small number jobs is one that only has so much credibility. Governments should no more subsidize their arms business than any other industry to safeguard jobs. Sir Samuel Brittan, the British economist and journalist, has written extensively on the weakness of the employment argument.

He says the argument is based on the myth that there is a 'lump of labor' that is engaged in making specific products, that cannot be deployed elsewhere. If defense orders are lost, those people become unemployed and unemployable, runs the line.

Brittan points out that millions of people change jobs, find jobs or leave jobs every year. 'Indeed, it is almost certainly easier for arms workers, many of whom have a wide range of valued skills, to find new jobs... Where will the new jobs come from to replace those lost in exporting weapons? Other jobs, on a much greater scale, arose to take the place of hand-loom weavers [and] drivers of horse-drawn carts.'[7]

A report by the British Ministry of Defence and York University,[8] published in 2001, revealed that 40,000 arms export jobs would be replaced by 67,000 civilian posts if arms exports were cut in half, albeit at a lower average salary per job.

A case study of the closure in September 1998 of the Vickers Defence Systems tank factory in Leeds, cited in Ingram and Davies' report, revealed what creative thinking and investment could lead to. A project between the local council, Vickers and the employment service focused on the workers' skills and training to develop their job prospects. Thanks to the scheme, 8 out of 10 employees had secured either new work, training or had voluntarily retired within 12 months.

So why do governments subsidize their arms industries?

So if arms do not really create jobs nor bring significant amounts of money into national economies, why do governments spend so much propping up the industry?

The answer is perhaps the hardest challenge which anti-arms trade activists face. Countries have a right to defend themselves, the argument runs, and government subsidy for the arms industry means they have the ability to buy weapons to do that. Citing possible future threats, governments argue they need to maintain a Defense Industrial Base (DIB).

The DIB is the ability of a country to manufacture, internally, the weapons and equipment necessary to arm their own military. Governments need to reckon on being able to arm themselves if they become cut off from overseas suppliers. They argue, for the same reason, the need to retain the technical expertise to build higher specification weapons in the future.

Governments support their arms industries by internal procurement (even if foreign weapons are cheaper), by subsidies and by promotion, so that in a time of crisis, the industry and the technological expertise still exists in the country and can provide for the government's military needs. By promoting and

Does government subsidy for arms exports harm national security?

There is a case to answer here, though it is perhaps not an argument that pacifist readers would want to make.

If arms companies do not have to compete in a true open market for the defense contracts of their host government, and automatically expect preferential treatment, they lose the incentive to produce better, higher spec weapons systems. The removal of government support for weapons manufacturers would increase global competition, producing an upward push in military technological advances.

Ingram and Davis argue that British internal defense procurement has a history of huge delays and of faulty equipment. 'The bottom line is that despite being subsidized by the taxpayer to the tune of around £4 billion ($5.8 billion) per annum, the British Defense Industrial Base (DIB)* is consistently failing to supply reliable equipment to our armed forces.'

The drive for votes and the safeguarding of jobs by creating 'defense pork', according to William Hartung of the World Policy Institute, has led to skewed spending in the priorities in the Pentagon, where 'crowd pleasing' technology has taken precedence over what the US really needs, thereby threatening security. ■

* The DIB is the ability of a country to manufacture, internally, the weapons and equipment necessary to arm their own military.

subsidizing exports, a strong domestic arms industry can be maintained.

This is a much-simplified explanation. Other reasons governments support their industries are because a strong defense industry is seen as a symbol of power in world affairs, because the arms industry has strong lobbying influence, and because politicians like to argue that they are safeguarding jobs since this wins them votes.

In practice, countries do tend to prefer their own industries when making decisions about what to buy for their own military. Around 85 per cent of arms bought for the UK forces are from British based firms.

The American defense industry's biggest customer is the US military, and so on across all major arms exporting countries, though BAE Systems' biggest customer is the US Department of Defense, because of the sheer quantity and value of arms that the US buys.

The picture has been slightly different in Europe in recent years because of the strengthening and growth of relations through the EU and because of strong competition by American defense contractors. The European arms industry has begun a process of consolidation across national boundaries, including the creation of major companies like European Aerospace Defense & Space (EADS), which supplies weapons across the region, as well as striking transatlantic deals. Europe has also entered into a number of joint production ventures, like Typhoon (Eurofighter), and even a single European armed force has been mooted.

The final result of this process may be a DIB on a European scale. Indeed, in 1996 an organization was set up to consolidate defense procurement across Europe. The *Organisation conjointe coopération en matière d'armement* (OCCAR), which covers Germany, France, Italy and the UK, is, according to German Defense Minister Rudolf Scharping in January 2002, 'the nucleus of an important European vision: a coordinated defense industrial research and development policy and a European procurement agency.'[9] In the meantime, the European partners are continuing to maintain their own DIBs by subsidizing and supporting their domestic defense industries.

Responding to a paper which attempted to expose how much the British Government subsidizes its arms industry, the British Defence Select Committee said: 'It could be argued that the costs identified are a small price to pay for making the political choice to ensure supplies by supporting strategically important defense manufacturing capabilities in the UK.'[10]

Anti-arms trade campaigners have found themselves needing to make strong arguments that the subsidies are so large they are not 'a small price to pay' for a DIB which is not necessarily needed in today's world. They have also had to argue that skewed government support for arms exports leads to other undesirable effects, not least human right abuses and conflict proliferation. They must also argue that the policy can lead to poor standards of weaponry and an inefficient arms industry. Finally they need to argue that diversification from arms manufacture into civil industry would be more productive in the long term (see chapter 8).

1 *Corporate Welfare for Weapons Makers, The Hidden Costs of Spending on Defense and Foreign Aid,* William D Hartung, World Policy Institute, August 1999. 2 *The Subsidy Trap: British government financial support for arms exports and the defence industry,* Paul Ingram & Dr Ian Davis, Oxford Research Group & Saferworld, July 2001. 3 'The ethics and economics of the arms trade', *RSA Lectures,* Sir Samuel Brittan, 28 March 2001, and also see sambrittan.com 4 OECD Trade Directorate statement, July 2001. 5 *The Subsidy Trap,* see 2 above. 6 'The Arms Trade as Illiberal Trade', Ann Markusen, Council on Foreign Relations & member of the Presidential Commission on Off-sets in International Trade, in a speech to Middlesex Conference on Economics and Security, June 16 2001, London, UK. 7 'The ethics and economics of the arms trade', *RSA Lectures,* Sir Samuel Brittan, 28 March 2001, and also see sambrittan.com 8 *The Subsidy Trap,* see 2 above. 9 OCCAR Battles to Establish Procurement Primacy, *Defense news,* January 21-27, 2002. 10 Defence Select Committee 2nd report 1999, paragraph 11.

6 Dirty deals

The problem of arms traffickers, mercenaries and child soldiers... The campaign to ban landmines... The arms trade, Afghanistan and the 'war against terror'.

THE TWILIGHT WORLD of arms dealing is intricately connected with a realm where people sell their own military might to the highest bidder. It is part of a world where children pick up guns and fight in wars because they've have never known anything but conflict and death.

It is a sphere in which unscrupulous traders will exploit what legislation there is to broker transactions between countries to turn a tidy personal profit. It is part of a world where arms companies will develop landmines and other 'area denial weapons' which, though not quite banned under anti-landmines legislation, still have the same effect of maiming and killing civilians indiscriminately (see chapter 7).

The world of the arms trade is one where terrible human tragedies, like the terror attacks of 11 September 2001, are seen as an opportunity to sell still more weapons and create a yet more unstable world. And the trafficking starts with the dealers.

Exploiting loopholes: the problem of brokering

Arms brokers are perhaps the most shadowy and murky of characters involved in the international arms trade. Operating usually on the very boundaries of legality, if the price is right, they arrange to supply weapons, usually small arms, to the most conflict-prone regions in the world. Brokers are the ones who spend their time on the telephone, organizing shipments from afar, often without having any direct contact with arms themselves. Traffickers are the people who actually shift the arms – transporting, or organizing the transport – but they are of course 'dealing' at the same time as they buy then sell on.

Operating through an intricate network of intermediaries, shipping agents, transporters, corrupt officials and secret contacts, brokers source the second-hand small arms, usually from stockpiles in central and eastern Europe and supply them to warring factions in Africa, Asia and Latin America. They might never see the arms themselves, and often work in such a way that a route from the arms can never be traced to them. Profits are posted in offshore accounts, front companies are set up and aliases assumed.

But a lack of international co-operation, political will and an ignorance of the extent of the problem means arms brokers can exploit loopholes in domestic legislation to go about their business with impunity.

There are thought to be several hundred arms dealers active in Western Europe alone, trading in leftover small arms from Eastern Europe. They operate illegally, bribing officials, faking documents and getting weapons smuggled, but they also operate with a veneer of legality.

In many countries, the traffic of arms only needs permission from the authorities if arms are to actually come in or go out of the country. Arms traffickers can be resident in one state and arrange an arms shipment between two foreign countries without any fear of punishment. In other cases, where laws are slightly tighter, arms brokers need only step into a country with weaker regulations to make their phone calls, have their meetings and arrange the shipments.

It has been well documented that arms supplied via brokers in Western states have gone to some of the world's most brutal conflicts and repressive regimes. The perpetrators of the Rwandan genocide in 1994 were armed by brokers based mainly in Britain, France and South Africa.[1]

One study concluded that only five states, Germany,

Meet the arms dealer

Mohammed is Lebanese and in his mid-40s. He lives with his wife and three children in London's wealthy Kensington district, works in a book-lined study and reads the *Daily Telegraph* and the *Financial Times* – both good for stock-market coverage.

'I got into the arms trade as an idealist,' he says, drawing on his cigarette. 'After the coup that brought the Ba'athist Government to power in Iraq, I was a consultant to the new regime. They needed weapons badly so they brought in a group of people including me. We just went right through – Britain, France, Italy, Germany – we got arms from them all.'

Mohammed has expanded his trade into other Arab countries, notably Saudi Arabia, where business is booming for middlemen. As with most arms dealers, payola – commission or bribes – is the key to his living. There would be no reason for Mohammed's existence if every minister and ministry were above board: arms dealers are used either because deals are shady – circumventing arms embargoes for example – or to allow government officials a healthy (illegal) cut.

A deal is usually initiated during a meeting between the 'consultant' and the minister at a plush hotel. The minister indicates the equipment wanted. The dealer then approaches the arms manufacturers telling them that if they appoint him as their agent, he will get them a contract in return for a percentage of the value of the transaction, which could be as low as three per cent, or as high as 15 per cent depending on how specialized the equipment required is.

Once an agreement has been reached and the minister has authorized it, an application is made to the government of the supplying country and, if approved, the transaction goes ahead. When payment is made the dealer gets his commission, normally splitting it with his mentor and possibly an official in the defense ministry who refuses to rubber stamp the deal without an 'incentive'.

'It's not the arms sales that are secret – it's the figures involved,' says Mohammed.

The British establishment has become rather touchy about arms dealers, embarrassed by a series of press revelations about shady deals being done in London. Britain is provider of arms, partly because the US Zionist lobby has prevented many sales to Arab states from Washington, which has forced the Arabs to go elsewhere. But Mohammed says it is also because the rules governing arms sales in London are more lax than elsewhere. If you ask an establishment figure these days about arms dealers they will tell you, 'I'm sorry darling, but there really aren't any.' Mohammed demurs. 'I think the figure is around 2,000 operating in London – 300 of whom deal in more than $50 million a year.' ∎

From the *New Internationalist*, issue 189 November 1988
by Janice Turner.

Sweden, the Netherlands, Luxembourg and the US, have measures that deal explicitly with arms brokering – even these vary in the extent of what they cover. The strongest legislation, in the US, requires that a US citizen wherever they reside, or anyone within US territory, must register and seek permission to be involved in an arms transaction. Even this process lacks transparency as the list of approved licenses and brokers is kept secret and so cannot be independently monitored.

A document on Small Arms and Light Weapons from the Organization for Security and Co-operation in Europe (OSCE), endorsed in late November 2000, explicitly addressed the need to regulate arms brokers. It recommended that governments require brokers to register their activities, that each deal is licensed and that full details of all parties involved are provided. But the document is weak on its definition of arms-brokering activities, and fails to mention traffickers or financiers.

The European Code of Conduct on arms exports does recommend information sharing and consultation between European states on arms control, but it doesn't include provision specifically on arms brokering. A Joint Action published by the EU in December 1998, which sets out to help solve the problems caused by accumulations of small arms, is considered only slightly stronger.

The Organization of American States (OAS) has adopted a series of initiatives tackling small arms proliferation, but they don't address arms brokering in a consistent way.

A United Nations Firearms Protocol is currently being drafted to 'promote, facilitate and strengthen co-operation among States Parties in order to prevent, combat and eradicate the illicit manufacturing of and trafficking in firearms, their parts and components and ammunition'. While this represents a positive step, campaigners argue that the best way to combat

What is an arms broker?

Arms brokers, arms dealers and trafficking agents can be characterized as follows:

- businessmen with military and security backgrounds and contacts;
- motivated by economic gain, not political considerations;
- use loopholes and weak regulations between national legal systems to conduct 'legal' but often unethical business via third countries;
- use transport agents and techniques to conduct clandestine deliveries to clandestine destinations;
- use complex international banking transactions and company formations in many countries, including in tax havens;
- locate sources of cheap, easily transportable arms for desperate customers in areas of violent conflict willing to pay high prices;
- rely on personal contacts and networks, not corporate identities;
- thrive on corrupt officials and weak law enforcement;
- sometimes fake documentation and use bribes, which can lead to involvement in organized crime. ■

The Arms Fixers – Controlling the Brokers and Shipping Agents,
Brian Wood and Johan Palema. A joint report by British American Security Information Council (BASIC), Norwegian Initiative on Small Arms Transfers (NISAT), and International Peace Research Institute, Oslo (PRIO), November 1999.

and control the illicit trade in small arms is to strengthen controls on small arms generally, including the legal trade. For more on controls, see chapter 8.

Mercenaries: the dogs of war

Selling arms is one side; purchasing people to use them is another. The use of privately hired might is nothing new.[2] The Romans used mercenaries, and the practice probably went back even before them. Italian merchants in the 16th century hired muscle to protect their assets and control trade routes. Colonial explorers were accompanied by hired fighters. From the mid-20th century, Western firms setting up mines and oil exploration in Africa, Asia and Latin America protected their assets by hiring armed heavies.

Mercenaries come under a number of guises, but all include the provision of military might or advice for a profit. Under the guise of 'security' for example, private military companies, consultants, advisors or training outfits, all manner of services to both governments and companies are supplied, including full participation in conflicts, the provision of arms, and armed protection of royal families and industrial plants.

Former members of security services often run modern mercenary companies, exploiting their contacts in the arms and political world. They hire disaffected, unemployed former soldiers wherever they win contracts, and source second-hand weapons and equipment for them to fight with. They will often provide whatever services are required, in exchange for hard currency or interests in mining and oil exploration.

UN Special Rapporteur Bernales Ballesteros was appointed by the UN General Assembly in 1996 to report on 'the use of mercenaries as a means of violating human rights and impeding the exercise of the rights of peoples to self-determination'.

He concluded that firms like Executive Outcomes (see box p98) 'have some mercenary traits but cannot be described as being wholly mercenary'. But he also said they were 'no less dangerous for the independence, economies, democracy and self-determination of the African peoples'.

The UK's Campaign Against Arms Trade (CAAT) said in a report on mercenaries: 'Ballesteros is right: [mercenaries] make things worse, not better. They encourage African leaders to seek military rather than political solutions, to engage in the zero-sum, winner-takes-all approach to politics that is the root of Africa's troubles. And the solutions they offer are at best partial and short-term.'[3]

Despite the proliferation of mercenary activity, and the problems it causes, no effective international legislation yet exists to regulate it. Several attempts have been made. Article 47 of the 1977 Additional Protocols of the Geneva Conventions contained so many criteria of the identification of mercenaries that it is legally

Executive Outcomes and Sandline

Executive Outcomes (EO), with its sister company Sandline, is a classic example of a private military company. The business was run by former security personnel, it was involved in controversial conflicts and it had clear connections in oil and diamond exploration.

EO was set up in South Africa in 1989. It was reportedly established under the leadership of two Special Forces officers Eeben Barlow and Lafras Luitingh. Both were reputedly former members of the notorious Civilian Cooperation Bureau (CCB), an organization which carried out the assassinations of the apartheid regime's more dangerous opponents. Barlow had corporate connections in Western Europe, including the British businessman, Tony Buckingham, who with his associate Simon Mann, is credited in setting up the company. Both were former British Special Forces officers.

Buckingham and Mann registered Executive Outcomes (UK) in 1993, and in 1996 established Sandline International, which was headed by Colonel Tim Spicer, another British Special Forces officer.

Buckingham was chair and chief executive of Branch Energy, which had mining properties in Angola, Namibia, Sierra Leone and Uganda. He was also the founder and president of Heritage Oil, which was deeply involved in the development of Angola's offshore oil drilling.

South Africans, among whom there were still many people poor enough to risk their lives for money, provided the military muscle, and Sandline/EO the organization and respectable front.

EO provided training, equipment and soldiers for the Angolan government's army in its battle with UNITA rebels after 1994. In March 1995, it was used by the then Sierra Leone government to put down an RUF guerilla insurrection, and protect mining facilities. EO has provided military training in Malawi, Mozambique, Botswana, Madagascar and Algeria.

After the overthrow of the Sierra Leone Government in 1997, the exiled President Kabbah and the Nigerian military enlisted Sandline to provide 'adequately equipped forces' to ensure Kabbah's restoration. The supply of that equipment, to the brutal and uncontrollable Kamajors militias, close allies of Kabbah, broke an EU embargo which forbade the supply of arms to any of the Sierra Leone factions. The incident led to an inquiry in Britain, following Sandline's claim that a UK High Commissioner had sanctioned the contract. ■

unusable. It was never ratified by France or the US.

A condemnation by the Organization of African Unity's Convention for the Elimination of Mercenarism in Africa in the same year criticized only those who bear arms against recognized governments.

The UN International Convention Against the Recruitment, Use, Financing and Training of Mercenaries 1989 has the same problem. It is so little regarded that only 11 states have ratified it and so it is still not yet in force.

CAAT wonders whether it is the close relationship between Western governments and private military companies which is the foundation for this reluctance to legislate.

After Sandline's supply of Bulgarian weapons to the pro-exiled government forces in Sierra Leone, one commentator wrote: 'Sandline and its bedfellows... have become a tool with which Her Majesty's Government can implement aspects of its policy that are best kept at arm's length.'[4]

In the Balkans, the US contingent of the NATO monitoring group in Kosovo is supplied not by the US army but by a commercial company called Dyncorp. When in 1995 a Serbian group in the Krajina district of former Yugoslavia refused to recognize the authority of the newly independent Croatia, they were overrun in days by a Croat force which had been specially trained by a US company, Military Professional Resources Inc (MPRI). The company also had a contract to train and equip the Bosnian army.

'These activities are undoubtedly in accord with US government aims in former Yugoslavia, and MPRI's board is full of recently retired US generals,' says the CAAT report, *The Privatization of Violence*.

Child soldiers

At least mercenaries can usually make their own choices; it is different for children. There are more than half a million children (under 18s) serving in armed forces, in more than 87 countries. At least 300,000 children are actively fighting in 41 countries, including Colombia, Sri Lanka, Sierra Leone, Uganda and Chechnya.[5] In some countries, very young children are used as messengers, spies and equipment carriers, but by the age of 10 they are given rifles, or rapid repeating machine-guns and set to fight in conflicts they cannot possibly understand.

As members of armed forces, children become lawful targets for attack, but the use of child soldiers also increases the danger faced by civilian children who come under suspicion from warring parties. Within armed forces, children are often treated brutally, suffering physical, emotional and even sexual abuse.

But it is not only faraway nations mired in internal conflicts that use child soldiers. The US is the country most opposed to setting 18 as the minimum age limit for recruiting and participation in armed forces. One in every 200 of its armed personnel is 17, while many more become temporary members as part of youth military training programs.

The UK continues to recruit 16-year-olds leaving school, and the recruitment process begins even while they are still at school. British soldiers under the age of 18 fought – and died – in both the Falklands/Malvinas

---

Double-take: two views of Wafic Said

1 'Wafic Said confirms £20m gift to Oxford'

Mr Wafic Said, the businessman and philanthropist, has confirmed that his gift of £20m, earmarked for a new building to house a world-class Oxford Business School, will go ahead if the University approves new arrangements announced this week.

The Chancellor, Lord Jenkins, said: 'This is a milestone for the University. We are grateful for this most generous benefaction – the largest private gift to the University for more than 50 years.

The Vice-Chancellor, Dr Peter North, said: `We believe this leaves us perfectly placed to launch a distinctive new management school that will produce the kind of internationally orientated, world-class managers who will tackle the global challenges of the future.'

Mr Wafic Said, already an established benefactor of academic initiatives and scholarships within the University through his Karim Rida Said Foundation, said he hoped the school would become a world leader, attracting the brightest and the best, both in terms of faculty and students. `It will be an ambassador for British business and, I hope, help to enhance Britain's competitiveness', he said.

University Gazette, 25 July 1996, 29 May 1997.

conflict and the Gulf War. Other countries that recruit under-18s to the armed forces, via conscription or voluntary enlistment include: Australia, Bangladesh, Belgium, Brazil, Burundi, Canada, Chile, Croatia, Cuba, Denmark, El Salvador, Estonia, Finland, France, Germany, Honduras, India, Indonesia, Iran, Iraq, Ireland, Israel, Italy, Japan, Jordan, Libya, Luxembourg, Mexico, Namibia, Netherlands, Aotearoa/New Zealand, Norway, Pakistan, Peru, Portugal, Republic of Korea, Sudan, Switzerland, Uganda and Yugoslavia.

A number of factors lead to the use of children as soldiers. Technological advances have made semi-automatic rifles light enough to be used and simple enough to be operated by a child, while rabid proliferation has made them cheap and easily obtainable. The longer a conflict goes on, the more likely children are to be 'recruited' as manpower becomes short – both young girls and boys are recruited – and new soldiers are needed to replaced the killed and injured.

2 'Oxford Business School funded by arms broker'

In the early hours of Monday morning, opponents of the new Said Business School in Oxford hung a large banner from the roof, proclaiming that the school was 'Built With Blood Money', due to a £20 million donation towards the school from businessman Wafic Said, best known for his role as broker in the Al-Yamamah arms deal.

Wafic Said is a businessman of Syrian origin, who was a key broker of the Al-Yamamah arms deals in which Britain sold weaponry to the oppressive Saudi government during the 1980s [see chapter 7]. The deal was the biggest known arms sale ever, and according to an award-winning BBC *Dispatches* documentary, it included fighter planes, as well as electro-shock batons which are used to torture political dissidents. The story of the business school has been one of buying approval from start to finish.

Said is able to exercise considerable influence over the business school, choosing half of the trustees himself. This is perhaps the most blatant example of why corporate influence over education cannot benefit the quality of learning, and we can only hope that other attempts to steer education towards the needs of business face the same stiff opposition. ∎

Corporate Watch, 9 November 2001.

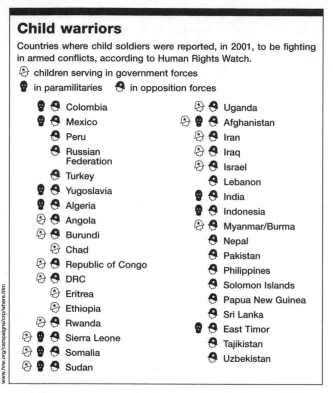

Child warriors

Countries where child soldiers were reported, in 2001, to be fighting in armed conflicts, according to Human Rights Watch.

⊕ children serving in government forces

● in paramilitaries   ◐ in opposition forces

● ◐ Colombia	⊕ ◐ Uganda
● ◐ Mexico	⊕ ● ◐ Afghanistan
◐ Peru	⊕ ◐ Iran
◐ Russian Federation	⊕ ◐ Iraq
◐ Turkey	⊕ ◐ Israel
● ◐ Yugoslavia	◐ Lebanon
● ◐ Algeria	● ◐ India
⊕ ◐ Angola	● ◐ Indonesia
⊕ ◐ Burundi	⊕ ◐ Myanmar/Burma
⊕ Chad	◐ Nepal
⊕ ◐ Republic of Congo	◐ Pakistan
⊕ ◐ DRC	◐ Philippines
⊕ Eritrea	◐ Solomon Islands
⊕ Ethiopia	◐ Papua New Guinea
⊕ ◐ Rwanda	◐ Sri Lanka
⊕ ● ◐ Sierra Leone	● ◐ East Timor
⊕ ● ◐ Somalia	◐ Tajikistan
⊕ ● ◐ Sudan	◐ Uzbekistan

Children are perceived to make obedient soldiers, they are cheap and are easy to manipulate. Children 'volunteer' or are coerced to join-up in order to survive, to prove their 'adulthood' or because it is a natural step in a culture of violence. In the Revolutionary United Front in Sierra Leone, children are held and trained for two or three months, threatened with death if they disobey orders or attempt to escape. In the Kamajors militias, they are initiated into secret societies and told they will gain magical powers and be immune to bullets if they join military forces.

Prevailing international law at the United Nations

sets 15 as the minimum age for military recruitment and participation in armed conflict, though there is widespread agreement that this age is too low.[6]

The Coalition to Stop the Use of Child Soldiers is an international movement of organizations seeking the adoption and implementation of an Optional Protocol to the Convention on the Rights of the Child (CRC) setting the minimum age for all forms of military recruitment and use in hostilities at 18 years of age.

By the end of 2001, a total of 92 countries had signed or ratified the Optional Protocol, but implementation will take many years and a great deal of effort. Programs to prevent child recruitment, including monitoring, providing alternatives, and establishing proper procedures, as well as programs to ensure safe demobilization and integration of former child soldiers are particularly needed.

Landmines: the legacy

Children, whether child soldiers or not, are often the main victims of landmines, perhaps the most vicious weapons brokered by the arms dealers. In the words of the International Campaign to Ban Landmines[7], 'Put simply, anything that landmines can do to an enemy's army, they can do to a civilian population. What they cannot do is discriminate between the soldier and the civilian. Their impact cannot be confined to the duration of the battle. Thus, under the laws of war, they are an illegal weapon.'

More than any other weapon of war, landmines have received much public and legislative attention over recent decades. They are horrific because their effects on civilian communities, after battles have ended, are so long-term and devastating.

Under internationally recognized definitions, landmines fall into two broad categories:

Anti-personnel (AP) landmine – 'A mine designed to be exploded by the presence, proximity or contact of a person and that will incapacitate, injure or kill one or more persons'.

Anti-tank (AT) landmine – A device designed to detonate by more than 100 kilograms of pressure.

Whether anti-tank or anti-personnel, the effect of landmines on civilian communities is the same. They kill and maim indiscriminately, taking children just as easily as heads of households. Families are devastated not only because of the loss of a loved one, but also because their means of income or a future generation is destroyed.

In the same way, those who are not killed when a landmine explodes are maimed or permanently disabled, becoming a long-term financial and emotional burden on families. Some landmines are designed to scatter thousands of shards of metal up to 50 meters, specifically to injure rather than kill.

Landmines also have devastating effects when they don't kill or maim, rendering thousands of acres of

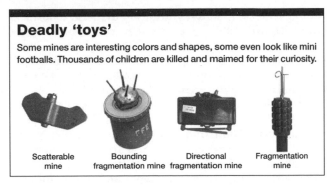

Deadly 'toys'

Some mines are interesting colors and shapes, some even look like mini footballs. Thousands of children are killed and maimed for their curiosity.

| Scatterable mine | Bounding fragmentation mine | Directional fragmentation mine | Fragmentation mine |

land unusable for farming or livestock. Families are forced to make a terrible choice between starvation or risking their lives on mined fields.

In Cambodia alone there are over 35,000 amputees as a result of landmines, and they are just the survivors. Mine deaths and injuries in the past few decades amount to hundreds of thousands. They are a daily threat in Afghanistan, Angola, Bosnia, Cambodia, Chechnya, Croatia, Iraq, Mozambique, Nicaragua, Somalia and dozens of other countries.

In December 1997, following decades of pressure from campaigners, a total of 122 governments signed the Ottawa convention, officially titled 'The Convention on the Prohibition of the Use, Stockpiling, Production and Transfer of Anti-Personnel Mines and on their Destruction'. Less than one year later the treaty became international law when Burkina Faso became the 40th country to ratify.

It is the most comprehensive international treaty of its kind, and became law quicker than any other treaty of its kind in history.

But despite worldwide support, and condemnation of the use, sale and stockpiling of anti-personnel landmines, a total of 53 countries still refuse to sign including China, Egypt, Finland, India, Israel, Pakistan, Russia and the US. The US's refusal has a devastating political influence, giving credence to other countries' refusal. The campaign continues to demand that these countries drop their opposition to the treaty, and to expand it to cover anti-tank mines and other 'area denial weapons' – a euphemism meaning they blow you up if you stray where you 'should not' – like cluster munitions and unexploded ordnance.

The 'trade' in landmines, as traditionally defined at least, is all but non-existent. Cuba, the United States, Russia, Egypt, Iran, Iraq, Burma, China, India, North Korea, South Korea, Pakistan, Singapore and Vietnam are still classified as producers of the weapons by the International Campaign to Ban Landmines, though some of them have only failed to prove written attestation to the contrary.

Military monitor *Jane's Mines and Mine Clearance 2000-2001* revealed there has been a 'virtual absence of mines – legitimate or otherwise – at arms shows and military equipment exhibitions this year' (though see chapter 7 on the DSEi arms fair). Thirty-four countries are known to have exported anti-personnel landmines in the past. All but Iraq have attested that they no longer do so. The trade in anti-personnel landmines has been confirmed to exist only in a relatively small amount of illicit trafficking.

For a book on the arms trade, it could be argued the issue should stop there – the trade in anti-personnel landmines no longer exists, and the manufacture is nominal. Unfortunately, the step is not so easily taken.

The Ottawa treaty covers only certain types of anti-personnel landmines, leaving vast loopholes where area denial weapons, including anti-tank weapons, remain available and traded.

The campaign against landmines concentrates now on encouraging the states who have so far failed to sign and ratify the Ottawa treaty to do so, but it has also broadened its outlook to the new and next generations of landmines and weapons that are landmines by any other name.

The weapon causing most concern for campaigners

is the cluster bomb. Usually dropped from a plane, it explodes just above the ground, scattering hundreds of miniature 'bomblets' over a wide area. Many of these bomblets fail to explode, remaining in the ground, just like anti-personnel landmines, until disturbed.

Like landmines, unexploded ordnance (UXO) poses a serious threat to lives and livelihoods. Between 1964 and 1973 the US dropped a huge number of cluster bombs over Laos. It is estimated that millions of unexploded bomblets remain. Cluster munitions were used in Kosovo and Vietnam, during the Gulf War, in the Falklands/Malvinas conflict, and during the recent attacks on Afghanistan. NATO admits to a failure rate of between 8 and 12 per cent in Kosovo, leaving as many as 35,000 live bomblets on the ground.

The campaign against landmines is far from won. Many countries, having signed Ottawa, pour money and research into mine clearance programs – an expensive and time-consuming business. But while taking mines away with one hand, the landmines of the future are being created and delivered across war zones all over the world. The arms companies which are earning millions from developing mine clearance equipment are also at the forefront of developing new generations of weapons, laying the foundation of devastation in the future.

The International Campaign to Ban Landmines is calling for a moratorium, banning the use of cluster weapons because of their devastating and long-lasting effects.

The 'war against terror'

No doubt landmines are playing their part in the current war on terror. Whatever one's opinion on the attacks on the US and war in Afghanistan waged in response, there is no doubt that the outcomes were good for the arms business.

'This event [is] all good things for the defense industry,' commented Richard Aboulafia, senior military analyst with the aerospace and defense Teal Group consultancy, one week after the attacks.

Immediately following the terrorist attacks on the US, stocks and shares plummeted worldwide as the markets reacted. But the value of shares in Lockheed Martin, the second biggest US arms company, rose by more than 30 per cent within a fortnight of the event. Within three weeks, shares in BAE Systems had risen by 7 per cent, in Northrop Grumman by 32 per cent and in Raytheon by 40 per cent.

Arms companies exploited the new 'threat to global security' with gusto. Northrop Grumman, maker of the B-2 bomber and the 'Global Hawk' unmanned sur- veillance vehicle, released a statement saying the company had the capability to 'meet current and emerging national defense needs, including anti- terrorism and homeland security.' David Polk, a spokesperson for Raytheon, manufacturer of the infa- mous Tomahawk missile, proudly announced, 'We are prepared to meet the urgent needs of our customers'.

The companies were not to be disappointed. The US Congress quickly announced a huge increase in military budget: $343.2 billion, an increase of $32.6 billion on the previous year.

As with the Gulf conflicts, arms firm Raytheon was an immediate big winner. Fifty of their million-dollar Tomahawk cruise missiles were launched on Afghanistan in the opening salvo on 7 October 2001. Britain immediately ordered another 48 missiles, in a $87 million deal. Raytheon also makes the infamous 'bunker-buster' bomb, a 5,000-pound missile used to tear apart caves and hideouts in Afghanistan.

Smart bombs

In the two months following the first bombing of Afghanistan, the US aerospace giant Boeing received orders for more than 1,074 'smart-bombs'. More than 4,600 of these were dropped on Afghanistan in the first few months. These are the weapons well known for missing their targets, including destroying a residential area near Kabul on 12 October 2001, killing 10 civilians. Three American soldiers were killed on 5 December when a smart bomb fell short of its target, and 5 Special Forces soldiers were wounded a week earlier in a similar miss.

But the 'war against terror' also opened wider the arms market to non-Western powers. In order to bring foreign nations on side, President Bush used military sales as a sweetener. He requested a blanket, 5-year waiver on military aid restrictions for all countries supporting the war. Congress refused, but agreed to consider waivers on a country-by-country basis.

Pakistan and India were the first beneficiaries. While the US didn't drop its embargo on 28 F-16 fighters imposed because of Pakistan's nuclear weapons program, the arms embargo placed on the country following its military coup in October 1999 was partially lifted. Pakistan agreed, despite huge popular opposition from its own people, to provide intelligence and liaison on the Taliban for the US and its allies.

Hawkish prime minister

India was one of the first countries to support the US's declared war on terror, leading to a comment by the US ambassador Robert Blackwill that 'we are at the beginning of a very important arms sales relationship' with the country. Prime Minister Blair of Britain quickly worked to secure a longstanding arms deal with India for Hawk fighter aircraft, even as he was urging the Pakistani and Indian leaders not to go to war with each other.

On 4 October 2001, less than a month after the New York and Washington attacks, US Secretary of Defense Donald Rumsfeld traveled to the Middle East, to put together a coalition against the Taliban. One of these countries was Oman, where Rumsfeld met the Sultan, Qaboos bin Said – the US wanted to use Omani airfields as a base to strike Afghanistan. By the end of the day, the Pentagon announced a $1.1 billion arms package to Oman, including 12 F-16 fighters, more than 100 air-to-air missiles, 20 Harpoon anti-ship missiles and radar equipment.

In exchange for Philippine President Arroyo's allowing US aircraft and ships to refuel on its military bases, the US prepared a package of equipment for the country including military transport aircraft, five military helicopters, 350 grenade launchers, 25 mortars, sniper rifles and surveillance equipment.

Yemeni president Ali Abdulla Saleh will now receive a potential $400 million aid package, which includes Special Forces training and US security assistance. Yemen has allowed the US to interview Yemeni witnesses and suspects relating to other terrorist attacks.

President Bush also announced new economic aid for Indonesia, amounting to more than $700 million including military training after President Megawati agreed to cooperate in the international coalition for the war on terrorism. Bush has also promised to lift the embargo on the sale of 'non-lethal' weapons to the country.

Israel, Egypt, South Korea, United Arab Emirates and Chile have also enjoyed confirmed or improved arms purchases following their support for the war against terrorism. The US has also managed to garner more support for its controversial National Missile Defense Shield program, despite the fact that the missile system could have done nothing to prevent the September 11 attacks, or a similar attack in the future.

1 *The Arms Fixers – Controlling the Brokers and Shipping Agents, ch 5, International Peace Research Institute, 1999.* **2** I am grateful to a CAAT report for the majority of material in this section. **3** *The Privatisation of Violence, new mercenaries and the state,* Campaign Against Arms Trade, March 1999. **4** *Defense Industry,* June 1998 **5** According to the Global Coalition to Stop the Use of Child Soldiers. **6** Protocols I and II to the 1949 Geneva Conventions and the UN Convention on the Rights of the Child. **7** www.icbl.org/resources/problem.html

7 The business of death

Bribery and corruption in the arms trade... The 'revolving door' and peddling political influence... Illegal deals at arms fairs.

JOE ROEBER, a British author and director of campaign organization Transparency International (TI), has said the arms trade is 'hard-wired for corruption'. It is a highly secretive business done behind closed doors. Government officials and arms company executives, from both buying and selling countries, go about their business away from the public eye, hiding behind the veils of national security and commercial confidentiality.

Though the trade is secret, the results of bribery and corruption are obvious. Invoices are inflated, and spurious administration costs are added to the cost of weapons programs. Generals and corporations lavish expensive hospitality on one another. Arms deals are signed which are well beyond the needs of the purchasing country, and more expensive than alternatives on offer.

The payment of commissions of one sort or another is widespread in international business, and until recently was even granted as a tax-free expense by many Western governments.

The negative results of such corruption and insider dealing are extensive. Developing nations purchase expensive systems they can't afford, diverting money away from health and education projects. Government policies on arms exports are skewed, and democracy is undermined, as lucrative 'consultancy' contracts are signed between weapons manufacturers and former ministers – or vice versa. And political parties gain unfair advantages by receiving huge sponsorship from arms producers on the unspoken promise of lucrative contracts after polling day.

When writing his book on the subject, Joe Roeber of Transparency International (TI) talked to arms trade insiders about corruption. Industry insiders, he reported, and many more knowledgeable outsiders confirmed that it is standard practice to bribe in arms deals.

The arms trade, bribery and corruption

'Far from being peripheral, corruption acts at the very center of the arms business, inflating what is spent on them and distorting procurement,' commented Roeber. 'The result is a waste of resources and an addition to global instability. That alone is bad enough. When the biggest losers are the developing countries, it cannot be ignored.'[1]

The US Commerce Department collects complaints from US companies about unfair competition from bribery by their competitors in overseas markets. More than half of all reports concern arms or defense equipment deals. The arms business is the most corrupt of all legal trades.

Bribery and commissions are close cousins, but must be separated. Few would argue that brokers, salespeople and experts should not be paid for their services in enabling a deal to take place – that is a commission, and is to a large extent legitimate. But it is when these commissions are ludicrously high, or they go to officials who have influence but no expertise, or they are lavished on many people who all have other interests in arms deals taking place, that bribery can be said to have occurred.

Bribery can be in the form of visible cash payments to officials, generals and government ministers; or in the form of gifts like expensive cars, gems or other kinds of in-kind donations. And it works in all manner of ways – arms companies will lavish gifts and commissions on decision-makers in purchasing countries to pursue a favorable outcome, but arms company executives often also receive their own gifts from purchasers to make the deals more favorable.

In the summer of 1999, a unique event happened in Sweden just prior to the country taking over the presidency of the European Union. The Swedish Ministry for Foreign Affairs organized an international colloquium on corruption in the arms trade. For the first time, representatives from the arms industry, government and military officials from 12 countries, academics and non-government organizations from around the world met in an open forum to address the subject.

Astonishingly, they soon agreed that the very nature of the arms trade made it ripe for corruption. It was an astonishing admission because the industry had traditionally been silent in the face of its critics on this issue, or had maintained the veneer of a clean, legitimate business, while carrying on insider-dealing behind the scenes. For the first time, industry chiefs, governments and the military were freely admitting that there was a problem of corruption in the business.

They gave a number of reasons why their trade was particularly at risk from corruption. The industry, for example, faces continued over-capacity in production, meaning competition between arms firms for orders is more fierce than in other industries. Likewise, because arms contracts are often large, but few in number, securing a deal can mean the difference between sink or swim for a weapons manufacturer.

The sheer size of orders also makes arms deals easy prey for corruption, because pay-offs and extras can so easily be hidden in multi-million dollar packages. And finally, the arms business is necessarily secret because it involves national security needs, which have be kept from competitors and potential enemies. This means both that deals take place without monitoring or scrutiny, and also that there is no 'market transparency' where deals can be compared with one another, and so overpricing and bribes cannot be identified.

It is no exaggeration to say that many involved in the international arms business do not see bribes, pay-offs and commissions as a big deal – indeed, they regard them as good business sense and will continue to pursue them as long as purchasers demand them.

But a wider examination quickly reveals that when corruption takes place to the extent that it does in the murky world of arms, it has some very real negative effects. In bribery there is always a loser, even if this is not immediately apparent as the dirty money is exchanged.

In developing and post-conflict countries, the problem is most stark. Bribes can motivate corrupt leaders to make superfluous arms purchases because they carry a kickback. Millions of dollars are squandered on weapons – money that the country desperately needs for development or genuine defense. The worst leaders will go further by cooking the domestic books to inflate the price of an arms purchase, while creaming off millions for themselves and their cronies.

Corruption also undermines the political, democratic and military systems. Bribery makes generals think more about their bank balance than about the soldiers they are sending to war. Corruption adds to the arms race, providing government buyers with incentives to buy more weapons than they require, and even in some cases, than they have military personnel to cope with.

Thankfully, arms-selling nations are coming round to the idea that corruption is a bad thing in the international arms trade, and are taking moves to rein it in.

For 25 years, the US has had anti-corruption legislation on the statute books. The 1977 Foreign Corrupt Practices Act (FCPA) bans payments to foreign officials, and to a large extent keeps corruption in US arms deals in check. But ironically, because few other countries have similar legislation, some have argued the move has led to a proliferation of corruption in non-US companies as they attempt to compete with sophisticated US weapons systems.

As Frank Vogl wrote in *Earth Times*: 'After all, generals may be a lot more tempted to pocket big bribes as

Deals with South Africa

The huge 1999 arms deal between the South African Government and European defense firms has been beset with accusations of bribery and corruption. Indeed, an inquiry set up in Pretoria to examine just some of the allegations, heard 43 separate specific accusations leveled at government African National Congress (ANC) politicians, officials and business people, ranging from allegations of gross incompetence to corruption and nepotism. By the end of 2001, three arrests had been made by South African police over the deal.

Allegations surrounding the deal include that the ANC chief whip, Tony Yengeni, receive a $46,000 Mercedes whilst chair of the Joint Standing Committee on Defense. The European Aeronautic Defense and Space Company (EADS) won $53.3 million worth of contracts to supply missiles and radar as part of the deal, and EADS is partly owned by Mercedes manufacturer Daimler Chrysler.

Joe Modise, former defense minister, and Shamin 'Chippy' Shaik, head of arms procurement, were also accused of pressuring bidding arms companies to use subcontractors linked to their families. One contract to fit electronics to new warships, for example, went to a Thomson CSF (now renamed Thales) subsidiary, African Defense Systems (ADS). Mr Shalk's wife is a senior executive at the company, and his brother is a director of both ADS and Thomson.

Links have also been made between contracts granted to British BAE Systems and the funding of overseas trips for cabinet ministers and senior MPs. Before BAE's Hawk was selected, cheaper and more modern Italian aircraft had been the preferred option for the South African airforce.

In the summer of 2001, the South African parliament launched an investigation into the allegations, albeit with a narrow remit, and was supported by ANC politicians. But in January 2002, four senior ANC ministers called a press conference to say there was no evidence of corruption in the deal. President Thabo Mbeki said the inquiry should be narrowed even further, and ordered the resignation of Judge William Heath, who was spearheading it. Heath did resign, but refused to hand over evidence already gathered about the deal.

As a senior political analyst at the Institute for a Democratic Alternative in South Africa (IDASA) said, 'If there's nothing wrong here, why make such a fuss about it? Why not let the inquiry run along the lines that Parliament first intended?' (See also box p 69.) ■

www.smh.com.au/news/0102/06/world/world8.html

a result of buying old weapons systems from European manufacturers, than acquiring the most sophisticated systems that come without kickbacks attached.'[2]

In 1997, the Organization for Economic Co-operation and Development (OECD), drew up a set of standards to combat bribing officials in international business transactions, which 34 leading exporting countries signed. But few have yet incorporated the rules into domestic legislation. Britain particularly dragged its feet, arguing that national legislation already covers the issues addressed. But pressure from the US, following the 11 September terrorist attacks, led Britain to introduce monitoring of money channels as part of its controversial Anti-Terrorism Act, which came into power on 14 February 2002.

However the flaw in the OECD code is that it is to be controlled and policed by governments, who are themselves mired in the corruption and secrecy game that is the international arms trade, and thus may not necessarily be trusted.

Saudi Arabia – the classic example

The largest defense deal ever struck in British arms-selling history is also, perhaps, the world's most corrupt.

The first Al-Yamamah deal with Saudi Arabia, worth more than $29 billion, including the sale of Tornado and Hawk aircraft, spawned allegations of bribery almost as soon as it was signed in 1985. The UK Guardian newspaper featured an article in October 1985 headlined 'Bribes of £600million [$413 million] in jets deal.' The second part of Al-Yamamah, signed in January 1993, was also beset by controversy. The main reasons for the outcry are:

The sheer quantity of arms, especially fighter planes, purchased by Saudi Arabia in Al-Yamamah far outweighed the country's military need, and included more planes than its air force had the pilots to fly.

The *Independent* newspaper reported in 1997 that British Aerospace 'was the biggest contributor to the blood money fund' of £730,000 ($1.05 million) which averted the death sentence for two British nurses accused of drug smuggling in the country.

A Saudi critic and exile to Britain, Mohammed al Mas'ari, was ordered to leave Britain by the government in 1996 after pressure from the Saudi royal family and arms companies, because his presence was jeopardizing arms deals.

In October 1991 an employee of Sikorsky helicopter company filed a law suit complaining that he had been unjustly demoted for threatening to blow the whistle on corrupt and illegal dealings as part of the contracts. He alleged, amongst other things, that bribes had been paid to

Campaigners have called for an international, independent body to be set up, with firm powers to monitor corruption in international affairs, and which can hold guilty companies responsible with financial penalties. But if even the OECD rules are beyond the will of nation states to ratify, the idea of an independent body can currently be little more than a distant hope. For more on legislative measures, see chapter 8.

The revolving door

One of the highlights of the anti-arms trade campaigning year is the annual shareholder meetings of arms companies. As a token shareholder in around five different corporations, I relish the opportunity each year to ask difficult and challenging questions to

two Saudi princes to secure an order for up to 90 helicopters (from British Westland, and Sikorsky) according to the UK's *Independent*.

The *Guardian* revealed that Westland agreed to pay a Saudi agent a 9.5 per cent commission on a related deal, potentially worth $50 million – but the deal fell through.

In 1991 the same paper revealed that Colin Southgate, chair of British electronics company Thorn EMI, 'admitted to paying huge commissions' of 25 per cent on a $57.6 million Saudi arms sale.

A TV documentary in 1994 identified UK, Saudi and other businessmen who were paid over $14.4 million for helping to organize part of the deal. Allegations included that Mark Thatcher, son of the then British Conservative Prime Minister Margaret Thatcher, received commission payments of $17.3 million from the deal.

The then British Defence Procurement Minister, Jonathan Aitkin, stayed in the Paris Ritz hotel in 1993, paid for by the Saudis, a factor in the Minister's eventual downfall. It was alleged Aitkin was instrumental in securing the $7.25 billion second phase of Al-Yamamah.

Finally in 1989, the British Government instructed its National Audit Office (NAO) to investigate the deal and allegations. Three years later, the parliamentary committee concerned said it would not publish the report's findings. The chair even refused to supply the report to committee members, but assured them there was 'no evidence of fraud or corruption'. Despite Labour Party promises before coming to power in 1997, the NAO report remains unpublished, hidden from the light of day like so many shady arms deals. (See also box on Wafic Said, chapter 6.) ∎

board members first in a formal setting, then later over coffee and biscuits.

Just as frequent as campaigners' challenges to arms company executives is their retort that it is *governments*, and not them, that campaigners should target for criticism. It is governments, after all, that make the rules under which arms companies operate.

This classic rebuff is nothing more than a tactic for preventing protestors from spoiling the buffet lunches. It is founded on the idea that arms companies and government are completely separate, with the corporations at the mercy of legislators. It is far from the truth. Not only do weapons manufacturers wield political influence with their constant threat of job losses, but they also make financial contributions to political parties with the hope of commanding influence.

The distinction is further blurred by what has become known as the 'revolving door' – simply put, government ministers, advisers and senior members of the armed forces frequently move into the employment of arms companies and vice versa. The supposed wall between government and the industry has a huge gaping hole in it, in which a constantly revolving door has been established.

Tim Webb, an expert on personnel issues in the armed forces and former official of the British Manufacturing, Science, Finance union, outlines how easy it is for British government and Ministry of Defence people to move into arms companies in his book *The Armour Plated Ostrich*. For example in the ten years 1984-94, approval was granted for 1,838 senior officers in the Ministry of Defence to take up defense industry employment.

The government Chief of Defence staff during the late 1980s, Sir Peter Harding, was appointed deputy chairman of arms firm GEC-Marconi. Former Minister of Defence Procurement, Jonathan Aitkin, was also acquired by GEC as an 'adviser'.

Sir Colin Chandler moved from a company which

was part of British Aerospace (BAe) to become head of the Government's Defence Export Services Organization (DESO), then transferred back to BAe as marketing director, before starting as chief executive of Vickers tank-makers in 1998. In 1995 Richard Needham, a government trade minister, was appointed to the board of GEC which later struck deals with Indonesia, a country Needham had worked closely with during his time in office.

Even today in Britain the revolving door continues to rotate. A former head of the DESO, Sir Charles Masefield, now sits on the board of BAE Systems (formerly British Aerospace) – by far the biggest seller of arms to the Defence Ministry and infamous for selling arms to repressive regimes. He once told me he helped the then Foreign Secretary Robin Cook write his infamous 'ethical foreign policy'.

In Frank Vogl's *Earth Times* article on bribery and corruption in the arms trade, he outlines how the George W Bush regime in the US takes 'this game of political pressure to an unprecedented new level'.

'Rarely before has US business taken such total charge of the Pentagon. Not only does the Secretary of

Defense [Donald Rumsfeld] come from big business, but so too do the new heads of the Army, Navy and Air Force… President Bush has nominated James Roche, a vice president at military aircraft seller Northrop Grumman, to become Secretary of the Air Force; Gordon England from arms and naval vessel manufacturer General Dynamics to become Secretary of the Navy.'[3]

For good measure, US Vice President Dick Cheney's wife, Lynne, serves on Lockheed Martin's board, a company which is a major contractor to the US Government and its allies.

The Stockholm colloquium on arms trade corruption in 2000 recognized the 'revolving door' syndrome as 'conducive to corruption in two different ways. Firstly, a government employee or military official may, in the hope or understanding of subsequently gaining a lucrative post in the private sector, be influenced to help get a procurement contract awarded to a particular company. Secondly, once a former military or civil service official does move on to a job with an arms manufacturer, the insider knowledge and personal contacts that he [sic] carries with him into the company environment may help to facilitate further corrupt deals.'[4]

Purchasing power

Donations from private companies to political parties and candidates are nothing new, and have been the foundation of many scandals for governments across the Western world. Not surprisingly, because there are lucrative domestic contracts to be won, and restrictive legislation to be challenged, the arms business is a major player in the cash-for-influence money-go-round.

As Lumpe and Donarski note in *The Arms Trade Revealed*, 'Whenever and wherever arms export policy is being made, financially self-interested representatives of the arms corporations are present. Generous campaign contributions from the weaponeer's political action committees (PACs) open doors, providing

Buying influence

Arms company corporate donations in the US, 1997.

	PAC* Contributions	Soft Money Contributions	Lobbying Budget[†]
Lockheed Martin	$590,960	$87,748	$1,900,000
Northrop Grumman	$336,075	$22,825	$3,594,197
Boeing Company	$183,119	$240,420	$2,900,000
McDonnell Douglas	$195,250	$135,372	$1,600,000
Raytheon	$229,950	$83,438	$980,000
Hughes Aircraft	$150,000	$6,175	$120,000

*PAC = Political Action Committee.
[†] The lobbying figures cover only the first six months of 1997.

The Arms Trade Revealed, Lora Lumpe and Jeff Donarski, Federation of American Scientists & Arms Sales monitoring Project, 1998.

access and influence on the policy making process.'[5]

According to the World Policy Institute, the 25 leading weapons-exporting companies contributed a record $10.8 million during the 1995-96 general election cycle in the US. Of this, $6.6 million came in regulated PAC donations and $4.2 million in unregulated 'soft' money – donations theoretically targeted for party-building activities, but often used to benefit specific candidates. Lockheed Martin was the leading arms corporate donor during this time. The Republican Party, more military-minded than the Democrats, received the bulk of donations.

As one arms industry lobbyist told *The Washington Post*, the rationale behind his organization's $5,000 contribution is pretty straightforward: 'When I call in the future, he [the politician] will know who I am.'[6]

Illegal deals at the arms fair

As already indicated, an arms fair is the hub of the weapons buying and selling business. It is at these exhibitions and conferences that corporate salespeople from all over the world meet tens, if not hundreds, of potential customers. In some cases deals are struck there and then, but much more often the seeds are sown for huge arms sales to take place in the future, away from the prying eyes of defense journalists and burdensome protesters outside the gates just waiting for the latest scandal to emerge.

These arms bazaars are indicative of how secretive and corrupt the business can be, and also of the lengths that companies and buyers alike will go to buy military, police and security equipment, even if doing those deals is against the law. Despite a huge number of controversial sales, allegations of dirty deals and illegal behavior at arms fairs all over the world, the fairs still receive only cursory monitoring from Western states, and no monitoring at all when they take place in the Near and Middle East and in the developing world.

Thank goodness then for investigative journalists who consistently reveal illegal and secret arms deals arranged during and after arms fairs. They supply arms campaigners with ample material to challenge governments to tighten up legislation on arms sales, and improve checks for illegal deals.

Flagship fair

DSEi – Defence Systems Equipment International – was supposed to be Britain's flagship new arms fair, replacing the lumbering Royal Navy and British Army Equipment Exhibition (RN+BAEE) with a sparkling new, slick-running private show representing the new government's approach to arms sales: clean, accountable, but still top of the agenda. The British Government contributed $362,500 (£250,000) to host foreign delegations.

But the slick, clean image of the DSEi defense exhibitions was not to be. Even before the exhibition began in September 1999, government sleight of hand was revealed when the Ministry of Defence (MoD) published its list of invited countries to the exhibition. Campaigners were pleased to learn the Labour Government appeared to have steered clear of inviting the most controversial countries (of course no country selling arms can be seen as innocuous). On the official list were Austria, Australia, Finland and Sweden.

Then the investigative journalist Yvonne Ridley, the same woman who was arrested in Afghanistan by the Taliban in late 2001, managed to obtain another list. The private company running the exhibition, PGI Spearhead, had secretly invited (after discussion with the British Government) a host of other countries of concern to human rights campaigners, including Morocco, Pakistan, Colombia and Israel.

More importantly, though, no less than two separate breaches of brand new British legislation banning the manufacture and sale of anti-personnel landmines occurred at and following DSEi 99.

On the third day of the exhibition, Campaign Against Arms Trade received a call from a researcher who had been working undercover at the fair. He said that a Romanian firm had brochures on their stall for anti-personnel landmines. CAAT arranged for a freelance journalist who had already been into the exhibition to go in the next day and check again for the material. He did discover the landmines information, and brought it out of the arms fair – to a waiting television crew.

The Romanian firm later told the British Government the information had been on their stall by mistake, but Paul Donovan (the journalist) told the film crew he had specifically been told the equipment could be supplied even though it was against the law. A MoD police investigation, which interviewed myself and Paul Donovan amongst others, failed to bring any prosecutions or even officially acknowledge a crime had taken place.

In December of the same year, it emerged that another arms manufacturer, Pakistan Ordnance Factories, had offered anti-personnel landmines for sale after meeting undercover journalists at the DSEi arms fair. The resulting documentary revealed the journalists were offered anti-personnel landmines, as well as thousands of small arms, for shipment to Sudan. Again, the British MoD police launched an investigation but no action was taken. The arms fair continues to take place in London every two years.

In May 2002, a journalist for the BBC's *Today* program, Andrew Gilligan, alleged that he too had been offered anti-personnel landmines for sale, by a senior executive of PW Defence, a UK company. Gilligan secretly recorded the offer. PW Defence's parent company, Chemring, immediately said the executive, David Howell, had been 'confused', and the company no longer sold the equipment in question. But defense experts Jane's had the item in its latest record of equipment for the company, which researchers said they checked thoroughly.

Chemring announced that Mr Howell had been 'withdrawn from duty'. The British police again said they would investigate the matter, starting with what they called an 'informal visit' to the company's factory. As this book went to press, the allegations of a breach of the UK landmines act were still being investigated.[7]

1 *Transparency International Newsletter,* June 2001.
2 www.earthtimes.org/apr/opinionbriberyandcorruptionapr30_01.htm
3 www.earthtimes.org/apr/opinionbriberyandcorruptionapr30_01.htm
4 Report from the Stockholm Colloquium on Corruption in the Arms Trade, Transparency International 2000. **5** *The Arms Trade Revealed*, Lumpe & Donarski, Federation of American Scientists and the Arms Sales Monitoring Project. **6** Quoted in *The Arms Trade Revealed*, Lumpe & Donarski, Federation of American Scientists and the Arms Sales Monitoring Project. **7** http://news.bbc.co.uk/hi/english/uk/newsid_1981000/1981157.stm

8 Containing the beast: regulation or abolition?

The United Nations, small arms and conventional weapons... The EU Code of Conduct on arms exports and US controls... The challenge of defense diversification... Challenges for the future?

MANY WOULD BE forgiven for feeling hopeless about the arms trade. The picture painted here is one of an uncontrollable, cash-eating monolith beyond the reach of individual nation states, causing havoc and destruction wherever it visits with no regard for human lives, decency, accountability or even the laws of the countries in which it operates.

Certainly the outlook is bleak. Next to prostitution, the arms business is perhaps the world's oldest and most ingrained profession. But ever since humans first traded weapons, there has been a body of determined, informed and passionate people campaigning for it to be monitored, controlled, curbed – and ultimately, for some – to be abolished.

A combination of research campaigning, monitoring legislation and government policy, letter-writing, public protest and direct action have slowly begun to bring changes. Campaigners cannot claim all the credit for the steps that have been taken locally and internationally. Sheer economic pressure and national security concerns have had their own role to play.

But campaigners can at least lay claim to much of the arms control legislation which has been introduced, and can continue the campaign for it to be tightened up, clarified, extended and renewed.

Whether the reader advocates the total abolition of the trade in arms, and on what terms that might take place if they do, is up to them alone. No-one should be under any illusion that total abolition, or even comprehensive reduction, could happen overnight – or even over a decade. Economic reality and international security make this no more than a pipedream.

However, what has already been achieved, as outlined below, can be built upon gradually by further well-informed, forceful and passionate campaigning. Every small victory brings a more just and secure world a little bit closer.

The UN small arms conference

'Perhaps the document is not going to be as strong as we would have liked, but it is a step in the right direction. It is a recognition by the international community that we need to do something about these weapons.' Kofi Annan, UN Secretary General.

In July 2001, an unprecedented event took place in New York. For the first time, representatives from 189 different nations came together under the auspices of the United Nations to draw up a Program for Action for tackling the problem of small arms, albeit only from an 'illegal/black market' emphasis.

Nearly 200 non-government organizations (NGOs), including groups from 26 countries affected by small arms, were on hand in New York to provide expert testimony and lobbying. For the first time, African and South American countries were given a real voice in the proceedings – even if the International Action Network on Small Arms (IANSA) had to pay for their air tickets to attend.

Preparatory committees had been positive. Here was a real chance to make internal steps towards reducing the proliferation of the illegal small arms trade. The Program drawn up would not be legally binding for UN member states, but it would certainly be 'politically binding' for countries all over the world.

Then the discussion moved behind closed doors. After two weeks of intense debate, the UN representatives formulated a Program of Action that fell well below the hopes and expectations of the NGOs waiting outside.

There were some positive outcomes, notably the increased emphasis on the humanitarian impact of the trade, including its effect on children and child soldiers. There was also what the NGO Saferworld called 'reasonably detailed provisions' for stockpile management, commitment to disarmament, and a recommendation that illicit weapons be destroyed.

But a coalition of states including the Arab League, China and the US worked hard at the Conference to ensure there were very few concrete commitments in the program. The US particularly insisted there be no ban on selling small arms to non-state actors, and no need for regulation of domestic gun ownership, even though most other representatives regarded these two as key to reducing the problem.

As Liz Clegg of Saferworld recalls: 'The issue led to a direct confrontation between the US and a number of African countries in the final hours of the Conference with the US apparently prepared to see the process fail rather than accept restrictions.'[1]

More generally, the final document was forced to include equivocal language, whereby states agree to 'consider' taking certain steps 'where appropriate' or 'relevant' and 'within existing resources'. The text was significantly weakened as a result.

Although the outcome of the Conference was only a feeble political binding, the meeting did at least set in motion international debate and action on the problem, with another Conference already scheduled for 2006. Like so much in arms control, small steps forward are better than nothing.

The EU Code of Conduct

On 11 June 1998, the Foreign Ministers of the 15 European Union (EU) member states adopted what is, arguably, the most comprehensive and progressive attempt to date to control and monitor the arms trade. The European Code of Conduct on Arms Exports aimed to set 'high common standards for the management of and restraint in arms exports from the EU'. It is a politically binding agreement, under which member states agree to abide by certain criteria when granting arms exports.

Amongst other provisions under the EU Code, member states agree:

- To assess the recipient country's attitude towards human rights;
- Not to issue an export license if there is a clear risk the weapons might be used for internal repression by the recipient country, or end user;
- Not to issue an export license if the export would provoke or prolong armed conflicts or aggravate existing tensions, or if the weapons would be used aggressively against another country;
- To assess whether the proposed export would seriously hamper the sustainable development of the recipient country;
- To assess the capability of the recipient country to exert controls on the re-export of the weapons to elsewhere, especially to terrorist organizations.

The Code was the product of decades of campaigning by non-governmental organizations and concerned politicians. The British Government, which held the EU presidency at the time, to its credit avidly pushed for adoption of the Code.

But like the UN Conference on Small Arms, the EU Code also fell well short of what campaigners had been hoping for. As it is renewed annually, they continue to press for it to be tightened up. One of the main concerns is about its lack of teeth or any mechanisms for enforcement.

The Code contains no clear legislation on monitoring and controlling arms brokering. As long as deals are not struck on EU members' territory, and the weapons do not touch their soil, the EU Code all but ignores the existence of the problem.

Nor does the Code provide a framework for a system of controlling where the armaments end up once they have been sold. There is no provision for end-use certification or verification. This is a glaring omission, since verification, follow-up monitoring and inspection should surely be an integral part of an arms control agreement.

There are many other problems with the Code, including transparency and scrutiny issues. In practice, it can clearly be shown not to be working, or at least to being very liberally interpreted. The British Government, its strongest proponent initially, has since 1998 exported millions of dollars worth of arms to countries which, according to campaigners, ought to have been excluded by the Code. These include human rights abusing countries such as Turkey, Saudi Arabia and China; to developing countries including Tanzania, South Africa and Kenya; and to countries involved in violent conflicts including Sri Lanka and Israel. The exports of other Code signatories follow a similar pattern.

Two months after a high-profile unveiling of the EU Code of Conduct, six of the EU's largest arms exporters pledged to co-ordinate methods of bolstering arms exports.

A US Code of Conduct?

Although the US has relatively strict legislation governing the involvement of its citizens in arms brokering (see chapter 6), the world's largest arms-exporting country has comprehensively stalled on drawing up its own code of conduct on arms exports.

Progressive Congress representatives have been attempting for nearly a decade to introduce a Code of Conduct on arms exports into US legislation. In 1995 International Relations Committee member Cynthia McKinned (Democrat) introduced the 'Code of Conduct on Arms Transfers Act' into the 104th Congress.

The Code allowed arms exports only to countries with a democratic form of government, respect for human rights, non-aggression against other states, and full participation in the UN Register of Conventional Arms.

A hearing was held on the bill in the Senate and the Code was voted on both there and in Congress. Although it was not passed into law, the votes represented the first comprehensive consideration of US arms export policy for 20 years.

Since then, politicians have managed to have aspects of the Code included in other legislation. The State Department Authority Act, passed in November 1999, contains Code-related language. It requires the President to begin negotiations on a multilateral regime on arms export criteria with other countries. It also requires the State Department to include in its annual report on human rights the extent to which states receiving US arms meet the proposed Code's criteria.

'While this is only a first step towards a US Code of Conduct, it establishes Congressional support for the Code principles and the need for greater restraint on arms sales by the United States and its allies,' says the Federation of American Scientists which co-ordinates a campaign for the Code.[2]

Other attempts to curb the trade

The Wassenaar Arrangement – This grew out of Cold War agreements to prevent the transfer of sensitive Western weapons to Communist East European countries. It now consists of 33 countries, including Russia, the US, many European states, as well as Australia and Aotearoa/New Zealand.

Wassenaar aims to 'contribute to regional and international security and stability by promoting transparency and greater responsibility on transfers of conventional arms and dual use goods and technology'. It set up a system of guidelines for export and information exchange between participants.

A 1998 plenary session of the Arrangement

approved methods of analysis and advice regarding accumulations of conventional weapons. It set out assessment criteria which may be applied to decide whether to export military equipment, including an assessment of the motivation of the buyer, regional stability, economic standing, human rights situation and the likelihood of destabilizing situations.

Like the EU code, Wassenaar requires member states to notify each other when they refuse arms exports according to the criteria, but there is no obligation on other states to follow suit. The whole denial regime is kept confidential. Campaigners have called for a no-undercutting policy to be introduced in Wassenaar and for the whole process to be made more transparent.

OSCE criteria – Prague 1992, participating states of the Organization on Security and Co-operation in Europe (OSCE) agreed that effective national control of weapons and equipment transfer was acquiring great importance.

At that time and in subsequent meetings, OSCE countries agreed on the need to ensure that arms transferred are not used in violation of the purposes and principles of the UN Charter. They also agreed to adhere to the principles of transparency and restraint in the transfer of conventional weapons; they affirmed their strong belief that excessive and destabilizing arms build-ups pose a threat to national, regional and international peace and security. Finally they agreed on the need for effective national mechanisms to control the transfer of conventional arms and related technology.

The West African Moratorium – The Declaration on Importation, Exportation and Manufacture of Light Weapons in West Africa, which covered not only illicit transfers, but also banned previously legal activity, was endorsed in 1998.

Only modest progress has been made towards its

implementation. Several states have applied for exemptions for specific arms transactions, and there is growing evidence of violations by states, notably those involved in the Sierra Leone tensions.

The UN Register of Conventional Arms – Launched in 1992, the Register was set up as an early warning system for identifying potentially destabilizing arms escalation, and to allow the international community to use diplomatic means to reduce regional tension and prevent conflict.

Member states are requested, but not required, to submit records in May each year of the arms they have imported and exported, and are invited to supply information about their domestic military holdings.

The main problem with the Register is that it does not require disclosure, and relies on the most transparent states to encourage others to follow their example. Another problem is that information is only supplied to the Register once weapons have been sold, meaning it cannot be used as a means of controlling the transfer of arms before they take place. The Register would be more effective if exports were registered at the time of order rather than delivery.

Finally, the Register does not monitor small arms, but only planes, tanks and other major conventional systems. Many nations suffer much more from the scourge of small weapons than they do from major battle systems. The landmines Convention is covered in chapter 6.

The challenge of defense diversification

Pushing for diversification into non-defense activities is one of the strongest tools for campaigners to wield in their arguments for the reform of the arms business.

Campaigners on many issues are often thrown by the challenge 'Well, what would we produce instead?'

The best response is that arms manufacturers and

related industries should pursue research, skill and expertise in creating equipment that does some kind of social good, or further modernizes society, rather than destroying it. This response also addresses peripheral challenges about job losses and economics.

Diversification implies changing governmental emphasis on arms production and sales into researching, manufacture and sale of non-military goods. It also implies diversification at a company level, a process where weapons producers invest money in creating civil goods, at the expense of their military interests, so that they gradually become non-military manufacturers.

In their report on British subsidies to the arms business[3], Paul Ingram and Dr Ian Davis set out a vision of what defense diversification might look like. They argue that it could take place throughout most aspects of the current arms realm, including aerospace, electronics, shipbuilding and engineering.

For manufacturers of fighter planes, for example, expansion into the civil aviation and space sectors are legitimate possibilities. 'Electronics represents perhaps the sector most capable of generating large-scale alternative civil markets,' the Report says. Defense companies that manufacture electronics for weapons systems could easily exploit markets in computers, office equipment, telecommunications, consumer goods, security, medical and environmental systems.

Globally, defense diversification is an idea that is unlikely to have its day in the near future. As an example, the British Government has set up a Defence Diversification Agency. But it receives only up to £2 million a year, and its remit includes brokering technology exchanges from the civil sector to improve military capability. There is no international interest, so far, in a global move towards manufacture of civil products instead of military equipment.

Beginning the debate on a global level is a realistically achievable target for arms trade campaigners.

Containing the beast: regulation or abolition?

Scrutinizing sales

A comparison of reporting and accountability in arms control legislation for a selection of European countries.

EU member state	Public annual report?	LICENSES				EXPORTS		
		Description items	Information on quantity and value licensed	Information on end-users of goods licensed	Information on licenses refused revoked	Description of items	Information on quantity and exported	Information on end-users
France	Yes	Description of 3 military categories	Value of exports disaggregated by country and further subdivided into 3 categories	None	Number of licenses refused under each EU Code criterion	Description of military categories	Value of exports disaggregated by country and further subdivided into 3 categories	None
Germany	Yes	Description of 22 military categories	Total quantity and value disaggregated by country	None	Number of refusals disaggregated by country, military list category/s and EU Code criterion/ia	None	Total value of deliveries of war weapons and value of commercial exports to ten most important recipients	None
Netherlands	Yes	2 military categories each divided into 10 sub-categories	Values broken down by country destination and military category	None	Destination country; description of equipment with category ranking; proposed consignee and end-user; reason for refusal, date, and denial number	Summary description of military equipment	Total global value of exports	None
Sweden	Yes	Description of 2 categories of military equipment	Total value per category	None	None	2 categories of military equipment	Total global value; value of exports by region and by country disaggregated by military category	None
United Kingdom	Yes	Summary description of the goods and/or military list rating	Total value of licenses disaggregated by country; and number number of licenses further disaggregated by license type	None	Number of refusals disaggregated by 8 categories detailing reason for refusal	2 categories: conventional weapons and small arms	Total global value of exports; total value of exports broken down by country	None

134

Immediate challenges

Campaigning against the arms business can sometimes be a game of getting a quarter when you have asked for a dollar. Though many organizations in the world are agitating for the complete abolition, and ultimately for a world without armed forces or aggression, many more are concentrating on more realistic and immediately achievable targets, as small steps towards a greater final aim.

The immediate steps towards abolition, should that be desirable, or at least a comprehensive overhaul of the global arms trade, fall into four main categories.

Transparency and accountability

One of the most important campaign priorities must be to persuade arms exporting states, and the arms business in general, to be more open, transparent and accountable.

Thanks to the EU Code outlined above, transparency and accountability have become an area of significant debate among EU members. The US already has far-reaching freedom of information protocols that go some way to revealing what goes on in the trade.

Transparency in export control policy is essential if governments are to be held accountable for their public commitments to peace, security and human rights. As the American non-government organization Arms Control Association puts its: 'A lack of transparency in arms export decision-making can lead to fears of human rights, regional security and sustainable development being overridden by pursuit of short-term commercial gain... Publication of comprehensive, detailed, and clearly structured annual reports on arms exports and establishment of formal procedures giving comprehensive information on the application of national export controls are key to ensuring the highest possible levels of transparency and accountability.'

Small arms controls

The second category is the urgent and desperate need to do something internationally about the trade, both legal and illegal, in small arms. As illustrated above and in previous chapters, this is a vital step which very few, even those within the arms business, would argue with. The UN Conference of 2001 was a vital step forward, and steps are now being taken to really tackle the problem through global and localized initiatives, with the support of governments, non-governmental organizations (NGOs) and people 'on the ground' in the worst affected countries.

Close legal loopholes for brokering

Another immediate strand for change in the arms business is to promote real actions to close loopholes in international, regional and domestic legislation

---

The Lucas Plan

In Europe, perhaps the most famous attempt at a company based initiative for arms conversion became known as the Lucas Aerospace Corporate Plan. In 1976, concerned that defense orders were dwindling and jobs might be lost, trade unionists and workers at the UK's Lucas Aerospace drew up a detailed plan for diversifying production to civil goods, with specific alternative products which could be manufactured.

Senior technologists and engineers at the company, assisted by academics and researchers, believed it was possible for the company to design and produce medical equipment, transport vehicles and components, new breaking systems, energy products and even undersea devices. Most goods they proposed had concrete social uses.

However the management did not want to know, and the then Labour Government failed to throw their weight behind the project. The plan eventually faltered, but as Tim Webb, a trade unionist and author on arms trade employment, recalls, one of the main problems was that the workers were ahead of their time. 'The ideas sparked by the Lucas initiative struck a chord well beyond the country's borders,' he said. 'It is still possible to meet trade unionists and others who work in the defense industries of many other countries who have not only heard of the campaign but have also attempted to emulate it.' ■

The Armour Plated Ostrich, Tim Webb, Comerford & Miller.

which currently allow arms brokers to go about their business with relative impunity. Evidence suggests that many of the arms transfers to the worst effected conflict regions and human rights crisis zones are organized and trafficked by arms brokering and transport agents.

Western arms selling countries are now gradually waking up to the problem of arms brokering, but the latest steps contained in the UN Program of Action on small arms, drawn up in July 2001, failed to set any comprehensive steps towards closing loopholes in national legislation. To some extent, introducing codes of conduct, tightening government to government transfers and even publishing clear and accountable arms export records can only be partially effective if arms brokers are allowed to continue their business unhindered.

Campaign for an International Code

Finally, the US President has now been instructed by Congress to pursue multilateral steps for controlling and monitoring the arms trade. There is a real possibility that within a generation, perhaps even before, an International Code of Conduct on Arms Transfers could be introduced, building on the EU Code. In 2000 the US and the EU signed a declaration to work towards a common vision on the question of arms export controls.

In May 1997, 14 Nobel Laureates met in New York to launch their own International Code as a first step to persuade arms exporting countries to adopt standards: 'Today, we speak as one to voice our common concern regarding the destructive effects of the unregulated arms trade. Together, we have written an International Code of Conduct on Arms Transfers, which, once adopted by all arms-selling nations, will benefit all humanity, nationalities, ethnicity, and religions.'[4]

Their proposed Code requires that arms transfers are only granted if transfer would complement and comply with international human rights standards, international humanitarian law, respect for international arms embargoes and military sanctions, promotes peace, security and stability, promotes human development and opposes terrorism. It calls too for public accounting of the Code's implementation, and transparent international co-operation through the UN and other bodies to improve and adjust the code as appropriate.

While the proposal needs updating to account for recent changes in the international arms trade, it is a bold attempt to set in motion some international moves to curb the arms export business. It is perhaps the best tool arms trade campaigners currently have to effect change on a global scale.

Keep agitating/join a campaign

Anti-arms trade campaigns have their own policies and priorities according to the national situation. Those with a specific interest should refer to the section at the end of this book to find their local anti-arms trade organization.

The Campaign Against Arms Trade in the UK, for example, had three campaign priorities in 2001:

- to end government support for arms exports, in the form of export credits, subsidies and marketing support;
- to introduce tough new export controls which included controls on licensed production and brokerage, as well as calling for greater transparency.
- to push for government to support a national move away from military production.

A broader view of campaigning

I think it is no exaggeration to say the world changed significantly in November 1999, when around 50,000 protesters descended on Seattle in the US where the World Trade Organization was holding its assembly. Protesters along with developing nations tired of being taken for a ride all but shut down the meeting, forcing the postponement of exploitative trade talks until a more remote venue could be found.

From Seattle onwards, politicians and executives of the biggest and richest transnational corporations realized that wherever they went, and whatever they did, an inspired, passionate group of united people was watching, criticizing and acting for social justice and equality.

Also for the first time, campaigners on widely diverse issues, from gay rights to third-world poverty, from peace and nuclear disarmament to environmental activists, joined together. They realized their concerns overlapped in many different and complex ways. They discovered that united campaigning, using the concerns they shared as a foundation, was more effective than disparate, isolationist campaigns along strictly issue-based lines.

The campaign against arms trading cannot, and should not, be considered in isolation from other concerns of social justice, except perhaps for convenience' sake. In almost every area of global injustice, the arms trade plays its deadly role. In earlier chapters it was revealed how the trade exacerbates conflict, promotes human rights abuses and worsens poverty in developing countries. The trade is also intimately connected to environmental destruction, inequality, immigration and asylum, gender and cultural rights, privatization and worker exploitation – in fact, most of the world's evils have their roots in the fighters, tanks, mines, guns and bullets that corrupt individuals and destroy lives.

As a consequence, there is now widespread concern about the potential damage caused by government insurance schemes, such as export credits (ECGs), for large construction projects like Turkey's Illisu dam. People are especially concerned because of the potential of human and cultural rights abuses in Turkey. The UK Government is 'minded' to grant ECG cover for the Yusefeli and Illisu dams, both of which are being built on historic Kurdish sites and will displace hundreds of thousands of Kurdish people. It is clear from this that export credits can be damaging altogether.

How similar is this issue to the provision of export insurance to arms companies that export weapons systems to countries that cannot afford to pay, or use the weapons to commit human rights abuses?

On the environmental front, in Liberia the rapid destruction of the rainforest is of concern to environmental campaigners because this is a factor contributing to global warming, as well as the loss of animal and plant species particular to those forests. How closely connected is this with the sale of small arms to Sierra Leone? Liberia covertly supplies small arms to the country using forest roads created by logging. Logging companies in Liberia sell gems acquired through the smuggling of weapons, to bribe officials to further their logging interests. And so the wheel turns...

This *Guide*, I hope, has illustrated how intimately connected the arms business is to a globally unjust, unequal and exploitative system. Curbing or even abolishing the international arms trade is just a small but vital part of working to make our world a more just, equal, healthy and safe place to live for everyone. Along with the protesters in Seattle, Prague, Genoa and elsewhere, anti-arms trade activists can exploit the connections between the weapons industry and global injustice to mount more effective campaigns.

1 IANSA UN Conference on Small Arms Report, IANSA 2001.
2 www.fas.org/asmp/campaigns/code/uscodecon/html **3** *The Subsidy Trap: British government financial support for arms exports and the defence industry,* Paul Ingram & Dr Ian Davis, Oxford Research Group & Saferworld, July 2001. **4** www.arias.org.cr/fundarias/cpr/code2.shtml – view the Code here also.

CONTACTS

International – European
**Network Against Arms Trade
(ENAAT)**
Umbrella group for European anti-
arms and peace organizations.
Tel: + 31 (0) 20 61 64 684
Email: amokmar@antenna.nl
Website: www.antenna.nl/enaat/
Amnesty International
Worldwide campaigning human
rights movement.
Tel: +44 (0) 20 7413 5500
Email: info@amnesty.org
Website: www.amnesty.org
**Stockholm International Peace
Research Institute (SIPRI)**
Conducts research on questions of
conflict and peace.
Tel: +46 8 655 97 00
Email: sipri@sipri.org
Website: www.sipri.org
**British American Security
Information Council (BASIC)**
Independent research organization
that analyzes government defense
policies.
US: Tel: +1 202 347 8340
Email: basicus@basicint.org
Website: www.basicint.org
UK: Tel: +44 (0) 20 7407 2977
Email: basicuk@basicint.org
Website: www.basicint.org
**International Campaign to Ban
Landmines**
Tel: +1 202 547 2667
Email: icbl@icbl.org
Website: www.icbl.org
**International Action Network on
Small Arms (IANSA)**
An international network of over 340
organizations from 71 countries
working to prevent the proliferation
and misuse of small arms.
Tel: +44 (0) 20 7523 2037
Email: contact@iansa.org
Website: www.iansa.org
Saferworld
Think tank on more effective
approaches to preventing armed
conflict.
Tel: +44 (0) 20 7881 9290
Email: general@saferworld.org.uk
Website: www.saferworld.org.uk

Australia – Australian Campaign
Against Arms Trade (ACAAT)
Tel: +61 7 4096 3236
Email: admin@acaat.org
Website: www.acaat.org/

Aotearoa/New Zealand –
Peace Movement Aotearoa
Tel: +64 4 382 8129
Email: pma@apc.org.nz
Website: www.converge.org.nz/pma/
Canada – Coalition to Oppose the
Arms Trade (COAT)
Tel: +1 613 231 3076
Email: ad207@freenet.carleton.ca
Website: www.ncf.carleton.ca/coat/
Germany – BUKO - Kampagne
'Stoppt den Rüstungsexport'
Tel: +49 421 326045
Email: rexbuko@oln.comlink.apc.org
The Netherlands – Campagne
Tegen Wapenhandel
Tel: +31 20 6164684
Email: amokmar@antenna.nl
Website: www.antenna.nl/amokmar
Spain – Campagne Contra el
Comerc d'Armes (C3A)
Tel: +34 93 317 6177
Email: juspau@pangea.org
Website: juspau@pangea.or
South Africa – Ceasefire
Tel: +27 11 339 1363
Email: stopwar@wn.apc.org
UK – Campaign Against Arms Trade
(CAAT)
Tel: +44 (0) 20 7281 2097
Email: enquiries@caat.demon.co.uk
Website: www.caat.org.uk
US – Arms Trade Resource Centre
(World Policy Institute)
Tel: +1 212 229 5808, ex 112
Fax: +1 212 229 5579
Email: hartung@newschool.edu
Website: www.worldpolicy.org/
projects/arms

Bibliography

*The Business of Death: Britain's
Arms Trade at Home and Abroad*,
Neil Cooper (IB Taurus, 1997)
*The Politics of British Arms Sales
since 1964*, Mark Phythian
(Manchester University Press, 2000)
The Armour Plated Ostrich, Tim
Webb (Comerford and Millar 1998)
Small Arms Survey 2001 (Oxford
University Press, 2001)
The Arms Trade Revealed, Lora
Lumpe & Jeff Donarski, Federation
of American Scientists & Arms Sales
Monitoring Project, August 1998.
*The Hidden Market: Corruption in
the International Arms Trade*, Joe
Roeber (New Press, September 2001)

Index